The Ultimate RPG Character Backstory Guide

"[T]his book is pure fun....Newcomers to the genre and returning heroes from past fellowships will find something in this for them."

—Horror Fuel

"It's not only a useful tool for building and fleshing out characters, it's also written in an incredibly entertaining way, making it a fun way to get the creative juices flowing."

—Gaming Trend

"It's akin to a graduate school course in role-playing games."

—Review Fix

The Ultimate Micro-RPG Book

"The ideas are brilliant, the breadth of content, completely creative."

—Borg

"Innovative."

—Nerdist

"[This book has] lots of play value."

—NPR Milwaukee

THE ULTIMATE

RPG

GAME MASTER'S
WORLDBUILDING
—— GUIDE ——

Foreword by Patrick Rothfuss, *New York Times* #1 Bestselling Author

THE ULTIMATE

RPG

GAME MASTER'S
WORLDBUILDING
—— GUIDE ——

PROMPTS AND ACTIVITIES TO
CREATE AND CUSTOMIZE YOUR
OWN GAME WORLD

JAMES D'AMATO
Author of *The Ultimate RPG Character Backstory Guide*

ADAMS MEDIA

NEW YORK   LONDON   TORONTO   SYDNEY   NEW DELHI

Aadamsmedia

Adams Media
An Imprint of Simon & Schuster, Inc.
100 Technology Center Drive
Stoughton, MA 02072

First Adams Media trade paperback edition May 2021

For information about special discounts for bulk purchases, please contact Simon & Schuster Special Sales at 1-866-506-1949 or business@simonandschuster.com.

The Simon & Schuster Speakers Bureau can bring authors to your live event. For more information or to book an event contact the Simon & Schuster Speakers Bureau at 1-866-248-3049 or visit our website at www.simonspeakers.com.

Interior design by Colleen Cunningham
Interior layout by Julia Jacintho
Interior images © 123RF

Manufactured in the United States of America

5 2023

Library of Congress Cataloging-in-Publication Data
Names: D'Amato, James, author.
Title: The ultimate RPG game master's worldbuilding guide / James D'Amato, author of The ultimate RPG character backstory guide. Foreword by Patrick Rothfuss, New York Times #1 bestselling author.
Description: First Adams Media trade paperback edition. | Avon, Massachusetts: Adams Media, 2021 | Includes index. | Series: The Ultimate RPG Guide Series.
Identifiers: LCCN 2021003371 | ISBN 9781507215517 (pb) | ISBN 9781507215524 (ebook)
Subjects: LCSH: Fantasy games--Design.
Classification: LCC GV1469.6 .D35 2021 | DDC 793.93--dc23
LC record available at https://lccn.loc.gov/2021003371

ISBN 978-1-5072-1551-7
ISBN 978-1-5072-1552-4 (ebook)

Thanks and Acknowledgments

Many of the game mechanics used in this book are based on the Powered by the Apocalypse game system developed by Meguey Baker and Vincent Baker. Some mechanics were also inspired by ideas in Brandon Leon-Gambetta's *Pasión de las Pasiones* and by the work of designers like Alex Roberts, John Harper, and Avery Alder.

James Mendez Hodes was hired as cultural consultant to assist in developing the exercise Making Magic.

Patrick Rothfuss and Drew Mierzejewski shared ideas during several wonderful conversations with me. Without them, many of the exercises in this book could not exist.

Contents

Chapter 1: Fantasy...25

Chapter 2: Sci-Fi...95

Chapter 3: Horror...135

Chapter 4: X-Punk...165

Chapter 5: Neutral...223

Foreword

I started role-playing back in 1984, way before D&D was cool. Luckily, I wasn't cool either, and immediately fell in love. I remember flipping through the *Dungeon Master's Guide*, finding the parasitic infection table, and being filled with strange delight at the thought of a world I'd never imagined before: a place of fetid bogs where the air and water themselves were perilous.

Since then, I've built so many worlds. Some for stories. One for a computer game I tried to write. Another for a high school novel. Many were for games I played with friends, or for games that never happened at all. Some of the worlds were no bigger than a single room, a town, a piece of river. Some were vast, fantastic, and thin as paper. Others were gritty, grounded, and apocalyptic.

In 1994 I started a new world and spent fourteen years expanding, refining, and revising it until my first book was published in the setting. And these days, it's not odd for me to be brought in as a consultant for video game companies or movie studios, usually to help them build worlds for their stories to live.

What I'm getting at here is that I've been doing worldbuilding for a long time. It's in my bones, and I do it the way other people knit or build model trains. If left to my own devices with nothing else to do, I'll invent magic systems, doodle maps, create imaginary currency systems....

Jump forward to 2018. I'm scheduled to make a guest appearance on a gaming podcast. I don't know much about the game, but I'm not worried. I'm pretty much a pro gamer. I'm OG with the RPG. I've thrown dice with Critical Role and the McElroys. I've played D&D on stage to cheering crowds of thousands (a fact that would baffle my younger self, and honestly still baffles me sometimes).

More embarrassingly though, I don't know anything about the podcast. This has happened a couple times. I'm doing too many projects. I'm exhausted and behind on everything. But it's too late to cancel....

I call in. Turns out the podcast is called *One Shot*. The host and game master is James D'Amato. And what follows is possibly the best RPG experience of my entire life. There were so many things I loved about that game. The system itself is a masterwork (it's called Kids on Bikes). The genre speaks to my heart. The other players were amazing performers who made delightful characters, but what truly stunned me was how gently and deftly James helped us build the world together. A unique, fully realized world, perfect for the story, created in about fifty minutes. It's a world I still remember and tell people stories about to this day. Since then, I've listened to more than five hundred episodes of James's podcasts, many of them multiple times. They've brought me immeasurable joy and expanded my horizons as a player, and storyteller, and worldbuilder.

And now here you are, holding his book. I think of myself all those years ago, flipping through the *Dungeon Master's Guide*, my imagination sparking. I remember that book fondly. It started me stumbling down a path I'd follow all my life. But it wasn't a great guide to where I wanted to go. It was rough, opaque, full of harsh rules and columns of numbers charts more suited to war games than stories. You are so lucky. With this book as your stepping stone and guide, I can't imagine how much easier your path will be. I can't imagine how much further you'll go....

—Patrick Rothfuss

Introduction

Maybe you're a new game master sitting down to create your first campaign. Or you're an experienced GM who's been playing role-playing games for years, and you're looking for new ideas. Perhaps you're a longtime RPG player flirting with the idea of becoming a GM, or a writer developing a novel or screenplay. In any case, allow me to be the first to congratulate you on your decision to create a world!

This book is here to help you on this journey. It'll show you where to start and what kinds of questions you need to answer. It'll show you how to make the rules that govern your new world work together and create challenges for your players without frustrating them. In this, you're not alone—thousands have done it before. So let your creativity run wild.

The Ultimate RPG Game Master's Worldbuilding Guide has more than thirty games and thought exercises to break down the world-building process. This makes setting development as easy and fun as playing one of your favorite games. We cover some of the most popular genres in RPGs: fantasy, x-punk, sci-fi, horror, and more. A few exercises will work anywhere. Together, they'll help you build the stage for your next great story.

You're about to embark on a journey in which you have unprecedented power. When you use your imagination to build a new world, you control everything: people, places, objects, history, and the fundamental laws of nature! The only rules you have to follow are those you agree to; the only ideas that matter are the ones you find interesting; and the most important tools are your influences and experiences. So relax, and get ready to explore a new world.

What Is an RPG?

A **role-playing game (RPG)** is a type of game in which players generate stories through shared imagination. It's a bit like the imagination games people play when they are young, games like "house," using dolls or action figures, and other simple games of pretend. These games all call on players to inhabit a role and interact in a shared imaginary space.

Tabletop RPGs published in game manuals introduce structure to this process. Published RPGs, or "**role-playing systems**," help players establish goals, track abstract information, and resolve conflicts. Rule systems and randomizers help adults make sense of what comes naturally to most children.

GMs and PCs

Everyone involved in an RPG is playing the game and is therefore a "**player**." When we refer to players in this book, we mean everyone at the table. Traditional RPGs have specific structural roles that make the game function. The most popular roles are **player character (PC)** and **game master (GM)**—note that not all RPGs have game masters.

What Is a PC?

In most games, the majority of people participating are responsible for controlling individual characters. For our purposes these characters *and* the people who play them are PCs.

Narratively, PCs are the protagonists. Players in the PC role are the primary authors of their story. PCs choose how their character thinks, looks, and acts. PCs interact with outside forces like other players and randomization, so a player in a PC role can't control everything that happens to their character. However, a PC always controls how their character reacts.

What Is a GM?

Many RPGs have a specialized role that controls any elements of the game that are not PCs. The title for this role varies, but here we'll refer to it as the game master (GM).

The GM is like a narrator, director, producer, supporting actor, and crew rolled into one person. We say GMs "**run**" the game. The GM is usually the arbiter of a game's rules. The GM is also role-playing. They control the actions of "**non-player characters**" (NPCs), which function to support or oppose PCs in the story.

For this book, the GM responsibility we care most about is controlling the world. The GM is not just responsible for the goblins in the dungeon, but also for the stones beneath their feet, the mountain over their heads, the sky, the weather, and the history of all those things. This is true in game scenes and between sessions; the process is called **worldbuilding**.

This book has helpful information for everyone, but it was designed with GMs in mind.

What Is Worldbuilding?

Worldbuilding is the process of creating places, objects, characters, culture, and history for a fictional setting. It also involves finding ways for concepts like these to exist in the same space. Effective worldbuilding makes a setting compelling, approachable, and clear.

Worldbuilding is about making choices. Big structural decisions like "Is there time-travel?" and "Do dragons exist?" Small decisions like "How many raiding groups are vying for control of the wasteland?" and "Does this monster have claws, teeth, or both?" Even seemingly insignificant decisions like "Is the bartender in a good mood?" and "Does this wizard read for fun?"

To some readers this might be a frustratingly broad definition. After all, that means *anything* you create could be an element of worldbuilding. My answer to that is "Yeah, I know; that's why I wrote this book."

Why Does This Matter for RPGs?

Role-playing is an improvised art form. Players build a story together. That story depends on players collaborating and expanding upon one another's ideas. The material you put into a game affects the material that comes out of a game. Strong worldbuilding makes it easier and more fun to play.

It's much easier to work with someone if you understand them. Anything is possible in fiction, because fiction is things that never happened. That also means the audience has to work to understand the material—to find reason in something that has full license to be unreasonable.

A well-built world presents themes and ideas to the audience in a way that allows them to follow the logic that governs the setting. It lets people know what's normal and what's weird, what to question and what to accept. That kind of clarity and approachability is essential for RPGs because the players are expected to contribute. If you feel like you don't understand what's going on, it's hard to collaborate.

Fictional worlds are also a kind of invitation for imagination. Did a book, movie, or TV show ever make you wonder about things you never got to see? Like the backstory for a side character, the motivations of a shadowy organization, or unexplored uses for someone's incredible powers? That is good worldbuilding drawing you in!

◉ Nothing's Ever Really New

Don't pressure yourself to create totally original ideas; they pretty much don't exist. Most of our favorite worlds were inspired by the work of other authors, mythology, real-world culture, or history.

In an RPG, strong worldbuilding makes a setting feel like an exciting toy. It shows players how all the fun ideas fit together and are waiting to be picked up.

Worldbuilding is a form of communication; it is another way to refine and present your ideas. When you collaborate with others, it is also how you present and honor *their* ideas.

Active Worldbuilding

We approach worldbuilding as a living process. You never really finish building a world you intend to use for storytelling. Every time you meet with your group for a session or write a new piece of fiction you're still worldbuilding.

When characters make decisions and drive action, their world needs to react. If characters can't change their world, then their stories don't have much meaning.

As a worldbuilder, you will constantly develop new elements for your setting until the story is over. The only difference between the worldbuilding you do to set the stage and the worldbuilding that occurs as the story unfolds is how much attention you devoted to it and the context showing why that information is important.

◎ **Make Investigations, Not Assumptions**

Be conscientious of how you use cultural and historical influences. Especially when they do not belong to you. Not everyone is equipped to understand what is representative and what is reductive. If you want to explore other cultures, understand and avoid stereotypes. That knowledge will make your ideas better.

If you approach your worldbuilding as an active process, it will make your life easier. You don't need to arrange every detail before you get the story moving. Even if you do spend hours developing the details of every plate and cup in your china shop, they are still going to shatter when you unleash the bulls.

Active worldbuilding provides you with a tool that is always at your disposal. You can discover and develop new ideas at any point in the storytelling process. At the end of the day the only thing that really matters is that your world supports the stories that interest you.

Everything Is a Canvas; Everything Is a Paintbrush

When we say worldbuilding, we mean the *whole* world. Big concepts like magic and space travel have an obvious effect on the stories. However, a single nail sticking out of a floorboard can change a misplaced footstep into a life-or-death struggle. You can add or change *anything* in a story, and any of those choices can be critical.

Worldbuilding Is Inherently Collaborative

While it's definitely possible to do a lot of worldbuilding as an individual, you probably aren't actually working *alone*. Even drawing on influences and using tools (like this book) are forms of collaboration. When you bring your world to your fellow players at the gaming table, you are collaborating. When you tie two of your ideas together, you are collaborating with *yourself.*

Support Your Choices

Ideas you put into your story only matter as much as you support them. A vampire assassin only really matters if it confronts the PCs or they discover its handiwork. A power surge only matters if it kills the lights and causes the PCs trouble. If you want something to matter in your world, support it! Ask yourself "How can I make this important?" and follow through by centering it in your story.

Work with Intention

Understand why you choose to include concepts in your world. If you don't have a reason for sexist gender roles to exist in your world, they don't need to be part of your story! Concepts like "realism" and "tradition" don't build your world; you do. The only good reason to put something in your world is that you want it to be there. If you know why you want to feature something in your game, you will be able to support it more effectively.

Don't Work Alone

You don't have to do everything as a GM. Even if part of your job description is controlling the world, you always have the option to outsource and delegate. You aren't required to invent a personality for a tyrannical general when you can copy Napoleon. You don't have to decide the name of a planet if one of your players has an idea. Choosing to incorporate external ideas is still worldbuilding. If you encounter difficulty, it might mean you are putting too much on yourself.

Look for Connections

Your ideas can actually support each other! The more connections you find between the concepts you and your players introduce to a world, the more cohesive it becomes. Deciding that the leader of a group of rebels is the child of the emperor they are trying to overthrow makes both the characters and their struggle more important. The more connections you can create between concepts, the more cohesive and alive your world becomes.

◎ The Solution Is Always More Books

If you would like more in-depth explanations of some of these concepts, you can find them in *The Ultimate RPG Gameplay Guide*, a previous entry in this series. It devotes whole chapters to explaining effective collaboration and creativity with intention. You get a lifetime of storytelling knowledge in 256 pages—what a deal!

How to Use This Book

This book is not an instructional manual. There is no right or wrong way to worldbuild. I'm not going to stifle your creativity by telling you to do things like me. This book is a toolkit, workbook, creative partner, and coach. It's here to make your process faster, more organized, and hopefully more fun.

Structure

This book is divided into five chapters. The first four are based on the most popular genres in RPGs: **Fantasy**, **Science Fiction (Sci-Fi)**, **Horror**, and **X-Punk**. The final chapter is designed to fit multiple genres; we called it **Neutral**.

Each chapter hosts a collection of exercises designed to assist you in creating world concepts for its genre. These exercises break down big concepts into small steps and use structured game mechanics to simplify the creative process.

Fantasy and Sci-Fi

These are broadly defined genres. We focused our exercises on helping you to make big decisions and generate useful world components. No matter how you want to approach these genres, there should be at least one exercise you can use.

Horror and X-Punk

For these more narrowly defined genres our exercises provide additional support. They explain why certain concepts and themes are essential to these genres while they help you develop them. This will help you make something that feels right, or identify which conventions you are challenging when you go a different way.

Some exercises you will use only once for each world. Others can be reused to create helpful details throughout your creative process. Every exercise will provide you with a piece of a larger picture. By tying those pieces together you'll create the foundational structure of your world.

Neutral

In putting together this collection we encountered concepts that felt like they had a place in multiple genres. Inspired by "Setting Neutral" RPGs, which provide rules that can be used to play in many genres, we created a "Neutral" chapter for this book! It has exercises that work with genres that have their own section and some niche genres that did not appear in this book.

Tools

This book uses "they/them" as indefinite and gender-neutral pronouns. Certain exercises call for the use of polyhedral dice. In those cases, a six-sided die will be called a "d6"; a ten-sided die will be called a "d10"; and so on. Some of these exercises call for playing cards; in these cases any standard deck will do, and the exercise will note if you should include jokers.

d20 Questions

These are short thought exercises to prepare you to create for each of the genres represented in this book. Roll a d20 and consider the questions posed to develop a sense of what you want out of your world or how to create the structures that define your chosen genre.

Priority System

Exercises using the priority system help you add complexity to simple ideas. They break down setting elements like characters, objects, and locations into their component parts. They task you with assigning priority to those parts. This ensures your ideas have strengths, vulnerabilities, assets, and complications. Simply assign priorities of 1 to 5 without repeating a number, and read the corresponding descriptions to get a basic outline for your ideas.

Prompts, Questions, and Choices

This book is full of prompts to inspire you. These are little ideas we're hoping you can use to create bigger ideas. Some are presented as lists that you are instructed to choose and combine one to three options from. In these cases, you can assume anything you didn't choose is not a part of your prompt. Many of our prompts are punctuated with open-ended questions to help you solidify and expand your ideas.

Tables

This book uses cards and dice as randomizers to generate prompts for tables. Simply roll or draw a card to generate a prompt or result. However, if something catches your eye you are welcome to choose.

Fantasy

Fantasy is one of the most iconic genres for RPGs. Almost everyone associates tabletop role-playing with medieval sword and sorcery. Despite that common association, fantasy is actually a very ill-defined genre. The umbrella term "fantasy" covers any setting that features mainly fictional elements.

Shakespeare plays like *A Midsummer Night's Dream* and *The Tempest*, classics like The Lord of the Rings and *Spirited Away*, ancient epics like *Beowulf*, TV shows like *What We Do in the Shadows* and *Avatar: The Last Airbender*, and even the mildly exaggerated reality of classics like *Treasure Island* are *all* fantasy. They all feel really different, though, because fantasy can mean so many things depending on the subgenre.

Our exercises for the fantasy genre are designed to help you make big choices and to support the "band of traveling heroes" theme that's popular in many fantasy RPGs.

d20 Questions

Our d20 questions for fantasy will help you narrow your focus so you don't get tangled up in too many possibilities.

 Roll a d20 for every player in your group (including yourself) and answer the corresponding questions:

1. Is magic present in this world? If so, how common is it?
2. What major event in this world's history is remembered largely inaccurately?

3. What happens to people when they die?
4. Which creatures are capable of speech?
5. What is special about the shape of this world?
6. What unseen forces have power here?
7. Is there a place here known for peace? Is it easy to find?
8. What mystery has gone unsolved for as long as almost anyone can remember?
9. What is something very commonly understood, and what is something considered secret knowledge?
10. Which landmark stands as a permanent reminder of a major event? Describe it.
11. How do people travel long distances in this world?
12. What is a relatively recent invention that dramatically changed this world?
13. What is considered rare and valuable? What is common and essential?
14. When not in person, how do people communicate? How has this method of communication affected society?
15. What fear is shared by many people across this world? What measure have they taken to guard against this fear?
16. What is something you wish existed in the real world that does exist in this one?
17. What annual event is celebrated in many different ways across this world?
18. How do the skies of this world look different from the sky we know?
19. What figure do people most commonly tell stories about? How are these stories told (books, plays, spoken word, broadcast, etc.)?
20. How important is technology to the daily lives of people in this world?

Making Magic

While it is never required, magic is a popular mainstay for fantasy settings. Some folks will pick up novels and RPGs just to see how magic works in a new world! Magic offers unlimited possibilities. For some people, that makes creating a magic system from scratch extremely difficult.

This exercise simplifies that process by adding structure. Choose from among the six paths of magic, and within each path you select, define six aspects to create an outline for your original system. You can develop as many or as few paths as you like, even doing some multiple times. With a few simple choices you will have a unique set of magic systems for your world!

The Six Aspects of Magic

For this exercise, you'll define the **source, cost, potency, commonality and accessibility**, and **pillars of mastery** for each path you choose to create. This exercise is mostly interested in the way your magic system affects story dynamics for PCs. Each of these aspects impact the choices characters make when using magic: what they need to use it, how they can grow stronger by using it, and how the world will perceive them as a practitioner. Every choice will yield interesting results.

SOURCE

This determines where magic comes from. Magic can come from objects of power or sacred sites; it can stem from the will of living and thinking creatures, be captured in a scroll or book, or exist in all things at all times.

The source of magic typically defines action that plays out when magic appears in the story. A conflict between two wizards can change dramatically depending on the circumstances; for example, are they using wands, shouting words of power, or chugging enchanted potions to access their power?

Sources also have a hand in determining what the practitioners of magic value, their aesthetics, and how they spend their time.

COST

Cost puts critical limitations on magic. Magic is a creative tool for players, and it can absolutely help them do whatever they want. However, if there is no cost for using magic, it takes tension away from the story. Defining costs helps magic fit into the story alongside other PC tools.

The cost of magic can be expressed physically, as in exhaustion, bleeding, and scars. It can be personal and metaphysical like corruption of the soul, shifts in emotion, or shortening of a life span. Cost can also take the form of external resources like magical ingredients, sacrifices, and even gold.

No matter how you define costs for magic, they become important levers for creating tension in your story. Compelling costs will make PCs seriously weigh their options when deciding to use magic, and lead to desperate efforts to scrape together resources to cast the right spell.

POTENCY

This helps you outline what affects the strength and effectiveness of magic. Some paths progress with the knowledge and skill of the practitioner, others depend on materials and equipment, and some are driven by environment and circumstance.

It's useful to have more than one factor controlling the power of magic. Sometimes the PCs will need to punch above their weight; sometimes you'll need a way to challenge an experienced party. Once you define what matters, you have the freedom to control if it is relevant in a given circumstance.

COMMONALITY AND ACCESSIBILITY

These are two different but related aspects. Together they shape who understands, controls, and uses magic in a setting. This lets your PCs know what expectations the world has of them and how open they can be about their abilities. It also tells you how much society may have developed differently because of the presence of magic.

Commonality determines how integrated into society a type of magic is. Some systems of magic are parts of everyday life, and some appear only for special occasions; some are available only to privileged classes, and some are hidden away in secret schools or exist only in story and memory.

If magic is part of a weekly cultural ritual, enables infrastructure like elevators or bridges, or wards off monsters and pests—it's a common thing even if not everyone practices it. If magic is used only by members of secret societies, is part of a distant history, or is forbidden within cultural norms—then it is not a common part of life.

Accessibility determines how easy it is for people to actually practice a type of magic. Some magic is available only to people born with special power. Other forms can be taught via various routes ranging from public education to specialized cloistered guilds. And some magic is available to virtually everyone to some degree.

Quiz

This quiz will help you make choices about the commonality and accessibility of different magic traditions. You should take this quiz for each tradition you develop. Your answers for a specific tradition might change to accommodate different regions and cultures in your world. Some questions can have more than one answer. Magic can be "rumored" for most people and "common" for privileged groups. Contradictions are fine as long as you know how they work!

1. Are people aware of this magic?
    1. Yes, as fact
    2. Yes, as stories or rumor
    3. Yes, but only privileged groups
    4. No, with few exceptions
    5. No, it is lost
    6. No, it is new

2. How integrated into society is this magic?
    1. It is a normal part of everyday life
    2. It is normal for special holidays and ceremonies
    3. It is reserved for certain milestones and special needs
    4. It is normal only for certain people
    5. It is separated from everyday life

3. Who can use this magic?
   1. Everyone
   2. Almost everyone
   3. Anyone who chooses
   4. Privileged people (common)
   5. Privileged people (rare)
   6. Almost no one

4. Is this magic considered acceptable?
   1. Yes
   2. Yes, in certain contexts
   3. Yes, in certain places
   4. No, with few exceptions
   5. No, it must be hidden
   6. Never

5. Is this magic respected?
   1. Yes, universally
   2. Yes, mostly
   3. Yes, in certain contexts
   4. Yes, in certain places
   5. No, with the exception of a few places
   6. No, with the exception of a few people
   7. No, universally

6. Is this magic regulated, controlled, or taught?
   1. No
   2. No, with few exceptions
   3. Yes, it is taught. By what entity? _____
   4. Yes, it is controlled. By what entity? _____
   5. Yes, it is regulated. By what entity? _____

7. Is this magic hidden or kept secret?
   1. No
   2. Yes, to keep practitioners safe
   3. Yes, to keep nonpractitioners safe
   4. Yes, to control power

PILLARS OF MASTERY

The source, cost, and potency of magic tell you how spells are cast and to what effect. Mastery tells you what separates a novice from a master of a particular style. It defines what the path of learning magic looks like.

It's important to understand mastery because one or more of your PCs will likely be following a path to mastery for their chosen traditions. The path to mastery has a basic structure for character narratives built in. It also defines the path powerful practitioners in your world have tread to get where they are—which can have a dramatic effect on their personalities.

This activity will call on you to answer questions and use your answers to develop conceptual "pillars of mastery." These are the most important conceptual skills for a practitioner to develop to become a master. These skills are best thought of in terms of broad ideas like "power," "scholarship," or "balance."

The pillars of mastery will be different for every path and will vary even among different disciplines on the same path. Your goal is to understand what high-level challenges separate "practitioners" from true "masters."

◉ All That You See Is Yours to Command

Don't feel the need to limit yourself to creating just one magic system for your world. Magic is often tasked with bearing the burden of many story themes. If it simultaneously represents the power of love and the danger of greed, its role starts to get muddled. Using a legendary system to represent the power of love and a forbidden system to represent the danger of greed will help divide these critical themes. That way your PCs can understand the consequences of their actions more clearly and play out their stories with intention.

The Six Paths of Magic

We have broken magic up into six paths with distinct structures. Depending on the needs of your world you might only want to develop a few. You might even opt to create multiple traditions within the same path. Read these descriptions and follow the steps to develop a magical tradition.

SCIENTIFIC

Scientific systems of magic represent the power of understanding and discovery. Characters who use scientific magic follow established processes to achieve repeatable results. These systems tend to look like alternative versions of real-world scientific disciplines involving similar methods like measurement, observation, and calculation.

Source

Scientific magic is unique in that it is the result of the interaction of natural forces. Like science itself, certain disciplines of scientific magic are applications of lessons derived from other disciplines. When considering sources, try drawing inspiration from real-world scientific disciplines.

Chemistry	Physics	Mathematics
Achieving magical effects through mixing elements and chemicals. Alchemy is a great example of scientific magic.	Magic that manipulates the interaction between objects and forces. This adds new laws to thermodynamics and creates new possibilities.	Rather than simply explaining the world through equations and formulas, mathematics-based magic allows people to manipulate the world through equations and formulas.

Biology	Astronomy	Engineering
Understanding and manipulating the properties of living things to achieve magical effects. Breeding magical plants and animals to create useful by-products.	Tracking and understanding heavenly bodies to manipulate or understand the world characters live in. Astrology is a great example of this.	Creating complex systems of interaction to build new tools. This usually depends on the interaction of several types of scientific magic.

Cost

☀ **Choose two costs for practicing scientific magic:**

- ○ **Precision:** This kind of magic requires precise calculations, and errors can be disastrous.
- ○ **Expense:** Materials and tools used to practice this magic are rare or valuable, calling for many resources to practice properly.
- ○ **Time:** Effects of this magic are not instantaneous. They involve lengthy periods of distillation, treatment, and other techniques to work properly.
- ○ **Complexity:** Even working with exact methods, there are variables that are difficult to account for and can corrupt the process if they are overlooked.
- ○ **Waste:** Use of this magic creates waste that is unpleasant or harmful, and disposing of it properly is a hassle.

Potency

✳ **Choose two factors that determine the potency of scientific magic:**

○ **Precision:** The more exact and meticulous a practitioner is, the greater the effects they are able to achieve.

○ **Material quality:** Ingredients vary in quality. The better your materials, the stronger their effects.

○ **Material volatility:** The more unstable and dangerous your materials, the stronger their effect.

○ **Scale:** Simply practicing your magic on a larger scale increases its power.

○ **Complexity:** The more elaborate your process, the greater your potential output.

Commonality and Accessibility

Complete the quiz in the introductory Commonality and Accessibility section to outline the role of scientific magic in your setting.

✏ **Then answer two of the following open-ended questions:**

● What is a folk belief or superstition related to this magic?
● What profession or institution depends on this magic?
● How has society developed differently because of this magic?
● What can these practitioners offer the world that others can't?
● Where might someone learn this magic?
● When would someone seek out a practitioner?

Question 1

_____

_____

_____

_____

Question 2

Mastery

Answer the following questions to help shape your concept of
mastery for this path:

- How is scientific magic usually learned? Can it be learned outside
  those systems?
- Is the idea of a master formal or informal? Can someone possess
  great power, knowledge, and skill without being respected as a
  "master"?
- Who is more respected: innovators or educators?
- Can a person become a master through scholarship without practical experience?
- Is any aspect of this magic still theoretical?

PILLARS OF MASTERY

Based on your answers, identify three pillars of mastery for
scientific magic in your world:

ARTISAN

Artisan magic systems are based on forms of expression and creativity. This is magic that exists in art, music, and the products of creative labor. These systems take real-world styles of art and tie magical effects to them.

Source

For artisan magic, you want your source to be something that takes care, time, and creativity. It should be something that would be a worthy endeavor even if there were no magic associated with it.

Music	Textiles	Writing
Arts based in rhythm, melody, and sound. Typically this sort of magic is less permanent and is based around moments of performance. This magic lends itself to collaboration.	Magical arts based on weaving, knitting, knotting, and embroidering fabric. It produces useful artifacts over longer periods of time.	Magic based around the creation and arrangement of words or symbols. This magic can come in the form of artifacts like spells and scrolls or be channeled to recitation like storytelling and poetry.

Sculpting	Painting	Physical
Magic based on shaping raw material like clay, glass, wood, and metal into artifacts. These can be art pieces like statues, wearable elements like armor and masks, or functional tools like weapons and vases.	Using paint, dye, ink, and other visual components to create magic in visual media. It can manifest as paintings, murals, tattoos, and comics. This magic has varying levels of permanence based on medium.	Magic based on artistic movement and performance. It can manifest as dance, gymnastics, and acting. It might provide kinetic enhancement, influence over the audience, or personal transformation.

Cost

☀ **Choose two costs for practicing artisan magic:**

○ **Time:** It takes a significant investment of time and patience to work this magic; very few things can be accomplished quickly.

○ **Strain:** Practitioners need to rest and recover to avoid injury.

○ **Emotional:** Artisan magic requires serious emotional investment from the practitioner and often leaves them exhausted and drained.

○ **Intricacy:** Spells using artisan magic require a complex interplay of different forces to work properly; even for masters these details are not always aligned.

○ **Material:** This magic often requires expensive tools and materials to work properly.

Potency

☀ **Choose two factors that control the potency of artisan magic:**

○ **Practice:** Each spell is an expression of the time a practitioner has spent honing their craft; they become more powerful as the caster becomes more familiar.

○ **Creativity:** The power in artisan magic is held in each practitioner's unique creative expression; even established spells and rituals depend on the caster bringing something personal to the table.

○ **Education:** There is a specific set of techniques that needs to be mastered in order for someone to have a full understanding of this type of artisan magic.

○ **Materials:** Practitioners are limited by the quality of their tools and materials. Even a novice will find greater power using higher-quality material.

○ **Intimacy:** The more personally and emotionally significant a spell is, the stronger it will be.

Commonality and Accessibility

Complete the quiz in the introductory Commonality and Accessibility section to outline the role of artisan magic in your setting.

Then answer two of the following open-ended questions:

- What is a folk belief or superstition related to this magic?
- What profession or institution depends on this magic?
- How has society developed differently because of this magic?
- What can these practitioners offer the world that others can't?
- Where might someone learn this magic?
- When would someone seek out a practitioner?

Question 1

Question 2

Mastery

✍ **Answer the following questions to help shape your concept of mastery for this path:**

- Is mastery over artisan magic permanent, or does it ebb and flow as a practitioner grows and matures?
- Does this discipline depend more on inflexible foundations or subjective creativity?
- Are masters limited by the same factors that govern the potency for other practitioners?
- Is a master more likely to influence their discipline through work or through teaching?
- What aspects of artisan magic can't be taught?

PILLARS OF MASTERY

✍ **Based on your answers, identify three pillars of mastery for artisan magic in your world:**

ARCANE

Arcane systems of magic are the most interested in dealing with magic as a concept purely by its own merit. Rather than adding magic as a result of real-world activities, it centers magic and creates systems of rules around it. Arcane systems focus on exploring themes of knowledge, power, and experience beyond the mundane.

Source

Arcane systems engage magic on its own terms. This means that arcane sources are usually based on conceptual and intellectual frameworks instead of existing real-world ones. They are fabricated solutions to support fictional concepts.

For sources like "birthright" it's very important to conscientiously engage with the themes that underpin the idea. There are plenty of foundational fantasy stories that use birthright models for magic, but they have ties to eugenics, theories of racial supremacy, and other negative ideologies. Understanding that connection will help you consciously avoid perpetuating harmful ideas in your own fiction.

Birthright	Truth	Emblems
Magic is rooted in the blood of the people who cast it. This source covers practitioners descended from magical creatures, chosen by fate, and inheritors of ancestral legacy. This works best in stories where a character's family history is important.	Magic relies on secret principles that govern the universe that are difficult for most people to perceive and understand. Attaining knowledge and understanding of these truths empowers practitioners.	Magical power is found in symbolic fragments like runes, words of power, symbols, and artifacts. These don't have to be visual symbols; they can manifest in sounds or thoughts, or in objects. The important thing is the power is contained in a thing and not in the practitioner.

Scholarship	Granted	Reservoir
Similar to that sourced in truth, arcane magic derived from scholarship puts power in information and fundamental universal mechanics. However, systems based around scholarship have advanced to the point that most essential truths exist in books and institutions—and can be claimed with study rather than discovery.	Magic power comes from beings with a stronger natural connection to magic. Practitioners worship, bargain with, or otherwise deal with these magical beings in order to attain arcane power. Typically the being granting power places limitations or caveats on its use. Practitioners are rewarded for knowledge of their benefactors or guile.	There is a physical or spiritual pool of power that exists in the world, and arcane practitioners must siphon from it in order to use magic. This type of source can limit power based on physical limitations of possessing magic material or the bandwidth of someone's access to a reservoir of magical power.

Cost

☀ **Choose two costs for practicing arcane magic:**

- ○ **Memory:** Casting arcane spells somehow damages or feeds on the practitioner's memories.
- ○ **Vitality:** Arcane magic saps a practitioner's health and energy. Going too far can cause exhaustion and even death.
- ○ **Ritual:** Specific conditions need to be met in order to access arcane magic.
- ○ **Mortality:** Casting arcane spells actively degrades the things that define practitioners as mortal creatures, causing them to slowly transition into new states of being.
- ○ **Sacrifice:** In order to satisfy the immense energies in arcane magic, the caster must provide external sacrifices, including food, valuables, blood, and even souls.

Potency

☀ **Choose two factors that determine the potency of arcane magic:**

○ **Age:** The more ancient the caster, the spell, or the materials used, the more powerful the effects of the magic will be.

○ **Will:** The limits of arcane magic are defined by the caster's own metaphysical fortitude and how they impose it on the fabric of reality. This can also be the collective will of a group of people all believing the same thing.

○ **Birthright:** There are powerful forces surrounding the circumstances of a practitioner's birth that determine their power. It might be related to bloodline, star signs, prophecies, or circumstantial omens—but something about a person's birth indicates their power.

○ **Knowledge:** The power of arcane magic is in some way a direct reflection of the caster's overall knowledge of the world. The more a practitioner knows, the stronger their spell.

○ **Secrecy:** Arcane power is partially determined by what a practitioner knows that others don't. Seeking knowledge and protecting it is the path of all truly powerful arcane casters.

Commonality and Accessibility

Complete the quiz in the introductory Commonality and Accessibility section to outline the role of arcane magic in your setting.

✎ **Then answer two of the following open-ended questions:**

● What is a folk belief or superstition related to this magic?
● What profession or institution depends on this magic?
● How has society developed differently because of this magic?
● What can these practitioners offer the world that others can't?
● Where might someone learn this magic?
● When would someone seek out a practitioner?

Question 1

Question 2

Mastery

Answer the following questions to help shape your concept of mastery for this path:

- Is mastery found in developing new ideas, mastering lost ones, or both?
- Are there limits on what a person can learn?
- Do masters tend to keep company with one another? With students? With the world?
- What skills pave the path to mastery? What lesson makes most practitioners falter?
- What roles do masters of arcane magic play in the world?

PILLARS OF MASTERY

Based on your answers, identify three pillars of mastery for arcane magic in your world:

NATURAL

This is magic derived from the forces of nature. Some traditions allow practitioners to manipulate nature, and others allow practitioners to draw power from natural systems. The source and how practitioners interact with it are critical to determining the character of natural traditions.

Source

Natural magic depends on forces that are outside human control but not outside human influence. Sources for natural magic might feel vast or influence the practitioner to adopt some of nature's wildness. Natural magic often forces practitioners to play by its rules rather than bending to the will of an individual.

When creating natural magic systems it's important to consider potential cultural appropriation. There are plenty of real-world belief systems that exalt and personify nature. Be careful when treading close to real-world ideas in your worldbuilding.

Elements	Flora	Beasts
Magic comes from the elemental forces that make up the universe and their interactions. This includes classic elements like Earth, Air, Fire, and Water—and unusual elements like Electricity, Light, and Gravity.	Magic comes from plants. It could be that plants need to be grown, cultivated, or foraged to collect magical by-products or refine inherent magical properties. It could also mean different types of magic exist within particular ecosystems.	Magic comes from beasts. This might be that beasts and their bodies create magical by-products, that beasts can be raised and bred for specific magical properties, or that natural magic practitioners have connections to bestial forms or powers.

Cycles	Positions	Spirits
Magic is determined by the natural cycles of the universe. They can be relatively short term like seasonal changes, longer term like geological or celestial epochs, or abstract like the cycle of life and death.	Magic comes from specific places in the structure of the universe. This source accounts for hallowed grounds and sacred sites, ley lines, and the movement of heavenly bodies influencing the world. All magic within this system is about finding the proper place and cosmic leverage.	Magic comes from willful forces that live within the natural world. They can take the form of powerful fey lords who rule nature, gods who represent specific natural forces, or spiritual beings that inhabit the many different facets of nature.

Cost

☀ **Choose two costs for practicing natural magic:**

- ○ **Control:** Practitioners of natural magic who are linked to their source risk losing themselves in this connection when they exploit it.
- ○ **Consumption:** Something of a practitioner's source must be consumed in the process of casting a spell.
- ○ **Vitality:** Natural magic demands energy from a practitioner or their source. This can be physical exertion, metaphysical life-force, or components of the body.
- ○ **Discomfort:** When drawing on the wild power of natural forces, a practitioner endures physical and mental pain related to the volatility of their source.
- ○ **Proximity:** To control different aspects of natural magic, practitioners must have access to their source.

Potency

☀ **Choose two factors that determine the potency of natural magic:**

○ **Cycles:** The power of natural magic depends on the ever-shifting conditions of the natural world. Certain spells, rituals, and ingredients will be powerful at different times.

○ **Environment:** The power of natural magic is tied to the state of the environment around the practitioner. A healthy forest might provide more power than a burnt forest, a frothing rapid might make magic more volatile than a gentle stream.

○ **Connection:** The deeper the bond between a practitioner and their source, the stronger their magic.

○ **Uniqueness:** Power is an expression of the diversity of the natural world, and what makes practitioners and sources strong is tied to individual distinction.

○ **Balance:** Natural magic thrives in stable systems where diverse forces create a harmonious whole. It is strongest when balanced or creating balance.

Commonality and Accessibility

Complete the quiz in the introductory Commonality and Accessibility section to outline the role of natural magic in your setting.

✐ **Then answer two of the following open-ended questions:**

● What is a folk belief or superstition related to this magic?
● What profession or institution depends on this magic?
● How has society developed differently because of this magic?
● What can these practitioners offer the world that others can't?
● Where might someone learn this magic?
● When would someone seek out a practitioner?

Question 1

Question 2

Mastery

Answer three of the following questions to help shape your concept of mastery for this path:

- Do masters need to fully commit their perspective to nature? Do they maintain a connection to civilization? Do they walk between worlds?
- Do masters take on aspects of their source in thought or appearance?
- Do masters change the world or preserve it?
- Who depends on masters of natural magic?
- What roles do masters of natural magic play in your world?

PILLARS OF MASTERY

Based on your answers, identify three pillars of mastery for natural magic in your world:

LEGENDARY

Legendary magic is an expression of the powerful themes at the heart of a world. It is the sort of magic that moves a story or defines the lessons someone should take from a story. It is more likely to use characters than to be used by them.

Legendary magic is typically more powerful than any other system of magic, while simultaneously being less practical. Characters in the world might have an understanding of the general nature of legendary magic, but it's not the sort of thing they can easily manipulate.

Source

Legendary magic draws on the foundational and ineffable laws of the universe. Sources for legendary magic are vast concepts that can actually benefit from being vaguely defined.

Irony	Fate	Poetry
There is an almost vindictive edge to magic. It works like a kind of retroactive moralizing force dealing out justice to evildoers and bittersweet rewards to tragic heroes. This kind of magic will ensure that two trees grow over the graves of star-crossed lovers and that misfortune finds the person who cuts them down.	Magic is the manifestation of the guiding hand of destiny. It shapes events through subtle influence more than overt displays of force. However, there is a sense of inevitability that makes it insurmountable. Fate pushes the universe along a course to meet the conditions of prophecy regardless of appearances or morality.	Magic stems from a kind of romantic storytelling logic. It is the reason true love's kiss can break a curse or a king's broken promise can topple an empire. This source works miracles that reinforce the core themes of a world.

Gods	Folkways	Axiom
Magic is the result of the divine. It follows the will and action of divine beings in a detached and impersonal way. It can manifest as powerful artifacts left over from creation myths, odd serendipity, miracle-working prophets, or overt deus ex machina.	Magic is tied to folk-tales and cultural practices of different peoples in the world. It follows the logic of myths and upholds the values of cultures at large rather than of individuals. This is the kind of magic that fuels the curse of an ancient king, or keeps a storm from ravaging a sacred temple.	Magic is the expression of cosmic principles through individuals. Practitioners manifest the power of the universe through their connection to it, seemingly defying natural laws. It is a profound connection to cosmic order.

Cost

Legendary magic is unique in that there is no cost associated with it. Other paths of magic have a reliable and transactional relationship with practitioners. By its nature, legendary magic cannot operate that way. Instead, there are narrative rules that govern its appearance.

☀ **Choose two rules from among the following that determine when legendary magic can enter the story:**

- **Healing:** Legendary magic appears to mend the broken pieces after a great struggle.
- **Faith:** Legendary magic is only available to those who are able to demonstrate unshakable belief in the underlying themes of the world.
- **Unlikeliness:** Legendary magic only appears based on a million-to-one chance. It creates certainty when something is extremely improbable but not impossible.

- ○ **Last hope:** Legendary magic appears when all other options are exhausted.
- ○ **Omnipresent:** Legendary magic is always present and working, but in ways so subtle that it appears absent.

Potency

Legendary magic is also unique in that it is always the most influential force when it is present. There are no factors that make it more or less powerful, just ones that determine how obvious and understandable its influence is.

☀ **When legendary magic appears, choose one of the following:**

- ○ No one can be sure it was present at all.
- ○ Only the wise and skilled see it for what it is.
- ○ Only the PCs understand it, and they must keep it secret.
- ○ Only the PCs understand it, and they must try to explain it.
- ○ It is obvious, dramatic, and undeniable.

Commonality and Accessibility

Complete the quiz in the introductory Commonality and Accessibility section to outline the role of legendary magic in your setting.

🖉 **Then answer two of the following open-ended questions:**

- What is a folk belief or superstition related to this magic?
- What profession or institution depends on this magic?
- How has society developed differently because of this magic?
- What historical event did this magic shape?
- What figure is associated with this magic?

Question 1

Question 2

Mastery

Legendary magic cannot be mastered in a traditional sense. These are elemental forces beyond mortal and occasionally even supernatural understanding. When a being assumes legendary power, they become a legend themselves. They feel less like an individual being and more like a vessel for the power and will of the universe.

✑ **Answer the following questions to help guide your understanding of mastery as it relates to legendary magic:**

- Have there been masters of legendary magic in your world? What deeds have they done?
- Are there any masters of legendary magic who are currently active?
- Do beings have to be "worthy" of legendary magic, or can it work through anyone?
- Can a being temporarily wield legendary magic, or does it require a permanent transformation?
- Does legendary magic typically solve or create problems?

FORBIDDEN

Forbidden magic is anything generally feared or shunned within a setting. It is dangerous for victims and practitioners alike, granting great power at a terrible cost. It is typically something people turn to in desperation or to do something the easy way. Generally it calls for behavior and morality that run counter to the core themes of your world.

NPCs are more likely to use this sort of magic than PCs. Occasionally PCs might have the opportunity to try it out, but that is often dangerous and harmful.

Source

Forbidden magic comes from dangerous places. When people say "There are forces better left alone," these are the forces they are talking about. The forces that govern forbidden magic are usually unknowable or hard to control, like beings that have a hidden agenda, behavior that falls well outside the ordinary, or natural drives that dull your thoughts—all things that tempt you to press your luck and potentially lose yourself in the pursuit of power.

◎ Behold the Nuance of the Dark Side

If you want your setting to avoid moral absolutes, consider developing forbidden magic as "taboo" but not necessarily wrong. Most characters will probably still shun or fear practitioners, but their reasons for doing so might be more complicated. The goal is for forbidden magic to be fraught but not necessarily "evil." Ask questions!

Does forbidden magic actually pose a threat or is it just easy to misuse? Who proclaimed this magical practice as forbidden and how do they benefit? What themes does this challenge and what themes does it uphold?

Alien	Sin	Adversaries
Magic coming from forces or beings fundamentally incompatible with the natural laws of the universe, like strange cosmic gods or hell dimensions. Engaging with this power challenges a practitioner's mental and physical well-being.	Magic is the result of transgression. Power comes from the breaking of natural and cultural laws. This includes engaging with taboo forces like death, and violation of specific codes. Practitioners are usually changed physically and metaphysically by this process, and those changes can be harmful.	Magic comes from malicious beings who grant power in order to corrupt the world. Unlike gods or spirits, there is something inherently corrupt in them. Their game is always to put everyone in a worse position, even when everyone gets what they want.

Appropriation	Passion	Desire
This magic comes from a power that rightfully belongs somewhere else. This source might work differently as part of another system of magic, but it changes after being used inappropriately. It likely works as a twisted mirror of its natural state.	Magic is the result of extreme emotional energy. The emotions at play are usually negative or positive emotions that have become toxic in some way. Practitioners cross key boundaries of control, making their power volatile and potentially dangerous.	Magic is the result of an individual's desire influencing the world. This is distinct from arcane will because desire here is not always intentional. This sort of magic grants wishes with ironic twists like a monkey's paw or a Midas touch.

Cost

☀ **Choose two costs for practicing forbidden magic:**

- O **Reason:** Forbidden magic disrupts a practitioner's ability to perceive the world, or opens them to a type of perception they cannot handle. This affects their ability to think and reason in line with the outside world.
- O **Morality:** Spells and rituals using forbidden magic actively change a practitioner's behavior and understanding of right and wrong.
- O **Transformation:** Practitioners of forbidden magic experience physical changes as they cast spells or become more familiar with occult taboos. These changes can be purely aesthetic, or painful and disabling.
- O **Blight:** Forbidden magic inflicts physical effects on the world around the practitioner. It might disrupt the natural growth and form of living things, create profane locations and objects, or weaken essential natural laws.
- O **Debt:** There is less necessary cost up front, but a sort of debt is incurred that a practitioner will have to resolve later. This might be an actual favor or material paid to an entity, or ironic misfortune.

Potency

☀ **Choose two factors that determine the potency of forbidden magic:**

- O **Transgression:** The power of a forbidden spell is directly related to the weight of the violations committed to cast it.
- O **Sacrifice:** The power of forbidden magic increases according to the value and importance of sacrifice made in order to cast it.
- O **Suffering:** Forbidden magic is stronger when it causes a greater amount of suffering.
- O **Woe:** Forbidden magic gains or loses power based on the general feelings of people near it. The greater the emotional unrest in the vicinity, the more powerful the spell.

○ **Perception:** Forbidden magic is powerful so long as people believe it is powerful. It becomes more potent based on the number of people who believe in it and the depth of their certainty.

Commonality and Accessibility

Complete the quiz in the introductory Commonality and Accessibility section to outline the role of forbidden magic in your setting.

Then answer two of the following open-ended questions:

- What is a folk belief or superstition related to this magic?
- What profession or institution depends on this magic?
- How has society developed differently because of this magic?
- What can these practitioners offer the world that others can't?
- Where might someone learn this magic?
- When would someone seek out a practitioner?

Question 1

Question 2

Mastery

✏ **Answer the following questions to help shape your concept of mastery for this path:**

- Is forbidden magic inherently evil, or is there potential for good? Should PCs have access to this magic?
- Is it possible to master forbidden magic without allowing it to control you?
- What threshold must a master of forbidden magic cross that most practitioners shy away from?
- Is there a known limit to the power of forbidden magic?
- How common is mastering forbidden magic?

PILLARS OF MASTERY

✏ **Based on your answers, identify three pillars of mastery for forbidden magic in your world:**

Pantheon

"Pantheon" in this context refers to the gods who inhabit or influence your world. Gods are a convenient way to call your PCs to action, add a layer of messy personal drama to world events, or justify interesting obstacles. They also give your themes literal personalities.

This exercise will help you create gods the way you would create a character in another game. Generate stats, assign abilities, and choose background details to create a cohesive pantheon where each god feels unique!

Domains

Every god needs an aspect of reality that they control or represent; we call this a **domain**. Usually domains can be summed up as simple concepts like "The Sea," "Lies," or "Wine." They influence a god's role, looks, personality, goals, and powers.

If you don't have a specific domain in mind for your god, roll a d6 and a d8 or choose from the following table. The d6 result gives you a general category for your god's domain and the d8 roll identifies a specific area within that category.

Natural	Cerebral	Celestial
1. A specific location	1. Mathematics	1. Stars
2. The Forest	2. Dreams	2. The Sun/Moon
3. The Sea	3. Imagination	3. Storms
4. Seasons	4. Strategy	4. Light/Darkness
5. Growth/Decay	5. Memory	5. Gravity
6. Beasts	6. Wisdom	6. Travel/Distance
7. Fertility	7. Truth/Lies	7. Nothingness
8. Food/Drink	8. Folly	8. Magic

Conceptual	Mortal	Elemental
1. Death	1. Kings/Queens	1. Fire
2. Time	2. Morality	2. Water
3. Fortune	3. War	3. Air
4. Order/Chaos	4. Art	4. Earth
5. Creation/Destruction	5. Any emotion	5. Nothingness
6. Freedom	6. Any profession	6. Electricity
7. Plenty/Famine	7. Fame	7. An atomic element
8. Destiny	8. Science	8. A specific object

Once you have your result, consider the needs of your setting and what role that domain plays in your world. Depending on the setting, the themes attached to a domain can vary wildly. For example, in a Bronze Age–inspired setting, the art domain might represent cultural ties and storytelling; in a Rome-inspired setting, the art domain might have closer ties to decadence and glorification of imperial power.

Aspects

For this part of our exercise, we have broken down attributes of the divine beings into five aspects: **power**, **interest**, **passion**, **form**, and **thought,** leveled 1 to 5. These aspects will help you define limits for the power of gods in your setting, shape their personalities, and help you create a pantheon of diverse beings that still feel connected.

When making a new god, assign a value from 1 to 5 for each of their aspects. To create a feeling of consistency when building a pantheon, choose three aspects: one to be a point of **major similarity**, one to be **minor similarity**, and one to **limit**.

The aspect chosen for major similarity will be the same for every god in your pantheon. The point of minor similarity will narrow the range of levels for a single aspect to one level above and below a single point. Finally, to create a limit, choose a level in a third aspect that gods cannot move above or below.

	1	2	3	4	5
Power					
Interest					
Passion					
Form					
Thought					

Your remaining aspects can be any level from 1 to 5 as you see fit! The following describes the five levels of each of the divine aspects.

POWER

Not all gods are created equal. Some are titanic forces that play games that rewrite the laws of the universe. Others play games with mortal kingdoms and shape events that change the world. Some grant mild fortunes to farmers who bring offerings.

1. At this level a god's power has a very narrow or specific focus. They might be the god of a particular tree, or command a single flock of birds. If they are tied to a concept, they might represent a specific shade of that concept rather than its entirety, like a "god of rhyming couplets" instead of a "god of art." They could even be an immortal servant of a force that seems vastly larger than themselves. They can grant minor blessings within their domain.

2. At this level a god's power might extend to dominion over a town or forest. They have a wide range of control within their domain, but it is usually conditional. They might represent a larger shade of their core theme like a god of poetry instead of a god of all art. They are still very much at the mercy of larger forces around them.

3. At this level a god's power can extend over large regions of the world or broad concepts. They might represent a powerful force like the wind or the sea. They can influence the world outside their domain, using their domain. These gods can produce miracles and forge artifacts.

4. At this level a god's power extends over entire planets. Should they desire they could rewrite the rules of their domain to suit their preference or impose the will of their domain to change natural laws entirely within certain areas. These gods can grant mortals extraordinary abilities that resemble the power of lesser deities.

5. At this level a god's power is cosmic, interwoven with the fabric of reality. They can reshape existence, forge new universes, and even create new gods. This level of power represents a far-reaching omnipotence.

This aspect determines the focus of a god's attention between the mortal and divine world. Some gods care only for divine matters, keeping their attention on their fellow deities and their heavenly domain. Some shun the divine altogether to think only of the plights of mortal beings and material things. Others split attention between mortal and divine, contending with the other gods for dominion over followers, earthly possessions, and heavenly domain.

1. At this level a god only has eyes for matters of the divine. They consider the mortal and material world to be entirely inconsequential. They do not even care for followers or souls. Their only concerns are their abstract domain and the actions of other gods. They might even be *overly* invested in the behavior of gods around them.

2. At this level a god will turn their attentions to mortal and material concerns only if they are forced to. If a rival or allied god cares for mortal and material things, they might use those things as leverage. However, it would never be their first instinct.

3. At this level a god values a balance between heavenly and earthly matters. They might see worshippers as a valuable status symbol, or prize material things within their domain. Heavenly matters are still crucial to their experience, and their ambitions are a complex web stretched between the realms.

4. At this level gods care far more about mortal and material matters than heavenly ones. They only think about other gods when it affects their own mortal domains. They are very present in the lives of mortals appearing to followers and interacting with them frequently.

5. At this level a god's only concern is for mortal and material things. They spend all of their time watching, influencing, and judging mortals. Their heavenly domain—if they even have one—is devoted in some way to mortal creatures or material desires. Their investment with mortals is always extremely personal. They rarely pay attention to the actions of the divine realm, even when it influences mortal matters.

PASSION

This aspect defines a god's emotions and will. Some gods are deeply invested in their ambitions, reacting to defeat with violent outbursts and success with exuberant celebration. Others are detached and almost mechanical in how they interact with the world with seemingly no desires at all.

1. Gods at this level are dispassionate and detached. Gifts and slights alike are met with impartial reservation. Even matters of their domain don't seem to move them.
2. At this level a god holds only a few things to be very sacred. Anything outside their specific interest is inconsequential. Without a deep understanding of their nature, they are nearly impossible to provoke into action.
3. Most gods at this level appear to be extremely capricious to mortals. This apparent fickleness can be driven by the general difference between gods and mortals. However, sometimes a god's passion is tied to their domain, waxing and waning alongside natural forces.
4. At this level a god is deeply invested in all matters relating to their domains. They are compelled to do more than simply maintain their domains; they want to expand or shape them. This leads to plots, conflicts, and sacrifices.
5. At this level a god is a torrent of forceful emotion and desire. They go out of their way to follow their whims and shape the world come what may. Their reactions are always extreme in ways that confound mortal understanding.

FORM

Gods have a vast range of possibility for form and presentation. Some are difficult to tell apart from mortals. Others appear as animals or objects. There are even gods that exist entirely as abstract concepts.

1. At this level a god's form is abstract and complicated in ways that defy explanation. They are all but impossible to behold and comprehend. These gods could appear as a number, a word, a complicated idea, or a collection of interwoven forces. Their body cannot be touched or beheld in a traditional sense.

2. At this level a god stretches the limits of a mortal's ability to comprehend form. They can be an undulating mixture of limbs, mouths, and eyes; an impossibly bright prism of dancing color; or a grand display of natural forces. The mortal mind struggles to make sense of these gods because they exist in an uncanny valley of the familiar and ineffable. Sometimes two mortals beholding the same god at this level will have different memories of its appearance.

3. At this level a god's form is unlike any living thing but still follows the rules of the material world. These gods can be stones, roads, statues, storms, and rivers. If it does have components of living creatures, they are mixed into unfamiliar displays, like a being with many animal heads and a body made out of wings and fire.

4. At this level a god has the form of a living thing like a plant or animal. If they have human qualities at all, they are mixed with other things, like a man with the head of a crocodile or a lobster with a human face.

5. At this level a god is almost indistinguishable from a mortal being. They might bear halos, unnatural tones of skin or hair, and other markers of divinity; however, that is not necessary. These gods often walk among mortals without notice.

THOUGHT

It is difficult for mortals to understand the will of divine beings. Some gods think in fundamentally different ways than mortals do. There are some gods that resemble mortals in thought and action, but even they are sometimes subject to ineffable whims.

1. At this level a god is so inscrutable to mortals it is hard to say they think at all. Everything they do seems random, counterintuitive, or so complex that it is impossible to understand.
2. At this level the god's thinking is understandable but only in themes and patterns. If a mortal understands the many intricacies of the god's domain, they might have some insight to its thoughts. Still, they do not behave like regular beings and make choices that even devout followers struggle to justify.
3. At this level a god thinks in ways more in line with beasts than humans. A mortal will most likely find the god's thoughts understandable, if unnaturally brutish or alien. They don't think like people, but it is easier to see how and why.
4. At this level a god appears to think like most sentient mortals with some very notable eccentricities. Perhaps they are too insistent on certain matters of social grace or they are too pliable with certain types of flattery. They are understandable—even reasonable—but with something seeming just a little off.
5. At this level a god thinks exactly like a mortal person. The only real separation between these gods and regular folk is that they also have the responsibility of managing a divine domain.

Aspects and Domain

Based on your god's aspects and domain, answer the following questions:

- **What is your god's name? Do they have titles?** Every god needs a name even if some don't like to bother with them. A god might also have titles like "Keeper of the Maze" or "Poet of Stars."

- **What heralds this god's presence?** Some gods are announced by processions of beasts; others by the sound of instruments, the smell of flowers, or flickering stars. What indicates this god's domain and status?

- **How does this god communicate with mortals?** Depending on their whims, a god can personally appear before mortals and communicate through prophets, dreams, signs and wonders, or avatars.

- **Where does this god spend the majority of their time?** Are they the type to sit on a throne, bask in a glade, command a thundering forge? Describe the markers of their realm.

- **What object is connected to this god?** It can be a tool, plant, food, or piece of clothing. This is something the god might hold, or their followers might use in a ceremony.

- **How does this god prefer to be worshipped?** Even gods who don't care for mortals have some idea of how to properly be honored. Do they like dance, songs, prayers, silence, sacrifices?

WHAT ARE THIS GOD'S RELATIONSHIPS TO OTHER GODS?

A strong pantheon carries eons of history. Gods form alliances, exchange insults, bear grudges, play tricks, fall in love, and so much more on scales that boggle mortal minds. To help you create a messy web of connections, choose two gods from your pantheon and decide if their relationship is positive, negative, or complicated; then roll a d12 on the following table and fill in the appropriate prompt.

	Positive	Negative	Complicated
1	___is a beauty unmatched in any realm. I will adore them until the end of time.	___stole from me. I will never forget.	___is a useful tool, but I feel no loyalty toward them.
2	___is my child, and they bring me pride.	___is honored in ways that are meant for me.	___ignores me, but I will force them to notice.
3	___taught me a lesson I shall never forget.	___imprisoned me.	___is my child with ___, and I cannot bear the memories.
4	I love to play games with ___ more than any other.	___destroyed something I love, and they will pay.	I love ___, who only has eyes for ___.
5	___is my protector, and I trust them.	___is an insufferable fool.	I depend on ___, but we cannot help but hurt each other.
6	___once made me a splendid gift, and I shall never forget.	If I had the power I would strike at ___ without hesitation.	___wants to teach me, but I think they are a fool.
7	I depend on the wisdom of ___ constantly.	I desire affection from ___, but they never offer it in a way that pleases me.	___was once lovely, but is slowly losing what made me love them.

	Positive	Negative	Complicated
8	I owe ___ a deep debt of gratitude, and it brings me joy to offer them thanks.	___ leads their followers astray and perverts the rightful order of creation.	I hurt ___ but have come to love them and cannot bear the guilt.
9	I am amused by ___ and wish to spend most of my time in their company to laugh.	___ cannot be trusted, and I have learned this lesson far too many times.	___ is moving down a dark path, but I feel it is my duty to help them.
10	___ commands much power and wisdom; it is right to pay them respect.	I do not like the way ___ treats me, but I believe I must endure it.	I do not know that ___ is not my child.
11	___ is dutiful and understands respect in a way few others do.	___ is too influential, and they are becoming a direct threat to my power.	I love ___. If I could, I would be them.
12	___ is my deepest and truest love; there is no me without them.	___ is my child, and they dishonor my name.	I must betray ___ though it pains me.

Make sure each god has at least two connections.

FOLLOWING

Even gods that shun the mortal world have followers who carry their word, tend their domains, and honor their names. In many cases PCs will interact with a god's followers more often than they will with the god itself. To determine a god's following, first add their power, interest, and passion together. The resulting number is the **faith** this god inspires. Then roll a d10 for each column in the following table. You may spend points from the faith pool to move results up or down one level for each point. A god's following is defined by **loyalty**, **influence**, and **size**, once you are satisfied or no longer have faith points to alter results.

	Loyalty	Influence	Size
1	This god is a bit of a joke; their name might appear in popular culture as something people appreciate but don't respect.	Even hinting that you follow this god loses you respect in both the mortal and divine realm. Any worshippers must keep their faith secret to function in society.	This church exists more on a conceptual level than anything else. The god awaits followers to come.
2	This god is only really important for academic interest. People know about them, but no one really worships them.	The most followers of this god could accomplish is writing a strongly worded letter.	This church only has one follower. The god rests all mortal matters on their shoulders.
3	This god's followers mostly use the god's name and associated power for their own benefit.	There is an organized religion of sorts, but it mostly exists conceptually. With great effort the followers can accomplish small things.	There is a small and dedicated group of followers loyal to this god and their domain.

	Loyalty	Influence	Size
4	This god is worshipped by a loosely connected following; much of their understanding of their own religion has been lost to time, and there is much debate over this god's will.	Followers of this religion are close to second-class citizens in most places. Even pooling resources, they don't have much more than the strength of their arms.	This is a single and modest congregation dedicated to this god.
5	Multiple sects worship this god but have deep-seated disagreements over how to interpret the god's will.	This god's followers are modest. They can build temples, make congregations, and mostly worship unmolested.	A few scattered congregations exist for this god around the world.
6	This god has at least one organized faith dedicated to them. Ecumenical politics still muddles the message from time to time.	This church has access to resources to provide support to followers just about anywhere, either from the pooled resources of a large community or from a few wealthy followers.	There are enough followers of this god to found a small nation.

	Loyalty	Influence	Size
7	Almost every worshipper within the church has a genuine dedication to this god and their domain.	This church is an important force in mortal politics. They can erect grand temples, spark conflicts, and easily protect the god's cherished domains.	There are enough followers of this god to populate a large nation.
8	Worshippers within this god's church are fanatical and willing to place their lives on the line in the name of their deity.	This church is a dominant cultural force. It commands nations on the strength of staggering resources.	Nearly every place in the mortal world worships this god in some capacity, even if they don't acknowledge it.
9	Worshippers submit their will entirely to the god, leaving almost no trace of mortal will remaining.	This church commands the fealty of other churches and even lesser gods.	Worship for this god has more presence in heaven than it does in the mortal realm.
10	All worshippers have internalized their dedication to this god so deeply that their every action is thoughtlessly bound to its desire. They aren't forced to worship; they are an act of worship.	This church is one followed to some extent by nearly all the gods in heaven and all the mortals on Earth.	Every being in every place across the mortal and divine realm worships this god in some capacity.

Sample Pantheon: The Gods of the Glas Isles

This region is populated by many scattered fiefdoms and is home to shepherds, fisherfolk, and squabbling feudal lords.

THE EAST WIND

Domain: Air

The East Wind is the first god of the Glas Isles. They exist not as a breeze but as a pattern on the wind. They wind around the islands, guiding ships from port to port and carrying fair weather. The wind is a divine force defined by movement. The East Wind cares little for those who offer trinkets to shrines around the isle. The East Wind's only desire is that things move, and they pursue that goal in an ever-shifting current.

Power: 2 | Interest: 2 | Passion: 3 | Form: 1 | Thought: 2

Following

Loyalty	Influence	Size
3	3	10

The East Wind is worshipped by all the gods and mortals of the Glas Isles. There are prayer mills set up on nearly every piece of land in the Glas Isles—when they move in a certain pattern folks know the East Wind is with them. This religion is not actually formalized, and worshipping the East Wind is more akin to a general observance of the divine. Gods and mortals who invoke the name of the East Wind do so more to justify their self-proclaimed divine rights rather than to actually offer praise to the wind.

Relationships

- Sportus taught me a lesson I shall never forget.
- Ignus cannot be trusted, and I have learned this lesson far too many times.

ABALON: THE BROKEN LOCK

Domain: Freedom

Abalon is fragments of iron that were once held inside Ignus. The East Wind felt the call of Abalon within Ignus and blessed Abalon's will to pull away. This allowed Abalon's yearning to give life to Sportus, who unearthed Abalon from the body of Ignus. Abalon wishes to break all forms of confinement across the Isles. Abalon has a more godly presence than Ignus and speaks to their followers in a voice that sounds like ringing iron. Anyone in possession of one of Abalon's shards cannot be restrained.

Power: 2 | Interest: 3 | Passion: 3 | Form: 3 | Thought: 4

Following

Loyalty	Influence	Size
7	6	3

There are seven shards of Abalon; they have sought to travel with folk who tire of the tyranny wrought by the petty Ríthe of the Glas Isles. The shards work in secret to dismantle the power of the Ríthe and free the people of the Isles.

Relationships

- The East Wind once made me a splendid gift, and I shall never forget.
- Sportus is my child with Ignus, and I cannot bear the memories.

IGNUS
Domain: Earth

Ignus is the second god of the Glas Isles. He is a stone that stands in the face of wind and wave seeking never to move, never to change. He lives in defiance of the East Wind, seeks to consume Abalon, and wants to destroy Sportus. He is a scheming and willful god that cares more about his place in the divine chain than anything else. He ineptly tries to manipulate what followers he has to meet his desires, but he lacks subtlety or grace. He is very human in thought and will directly speak with mortals in his presence.

Power: 1 | **Interest:** 2 | **Passion:** 3 | **Form:** 3 | **Thought:** 6

Following

Loyalty	Influence	Size
1	4	5

Ignus is something of a mascot for the Thirsty Widow, a tavern in Farraige Cloiche. He is displayed in the center of the pub, where he bloviates at any mortal drunk enough to listen. His image is stamped and embroidered onto merchandise of all kinds—though most people outside Farraige Cloiche see these items as tacky. Many travelers pass through the Thirsty Widow to see the talking rock.

Relationships
- Sportus leads their followers astray and perverts the rightful order of creation.
- I love Abalon. If I could, I would be them.

SPORTUS

Domain: Decay

Sportus is the youngest god of the Isles. They were born from Abalon, freeing themself from Ignus. Sportus is living corrosion, a fungal lichen that eats stone, flesh, and bone indiscriminately. They work slowly and steadily and cannot spread without the help of flowers of the will of the East Wind. Sportus thinks only as a fungus would think, desiring to spread and consume. Sportus cares only for the firmament, as that is what they eat. Sportus looks like an undulating blurry distortion that warps color; they can be seen but appear differently to various observers.

Power: 1 | **Interest:** 4 | **Passion:** 3 | **Form:** 2 | **Thought:** 3

Following

Loyalty	Influence	Size
5	1	5

There are a few scattered cults dedicated to Sportus across the Glas Isles. They all spread Sportus's form from stone to flesh wherever they travel. However, there is a sharp disagreement between existing factions on the proper way to worship decay. Some treat worship of Sportus as a part of the natural cycle of creation—destroying so new things can be built. Some seek only to spread Sportus without rhyme or reason. There is a doomsday faction that feels Sportus should consume all things. No matter the nature of their belief, Sportus cultists are often shunned because they bring destruction.

Relationships
- The East Wind is my protector, and I trust them.
- I hurt Ignus but have come to love them and cannot bear the guilt.

One Thing to Rule Them All

In fantasy, some conflicts revolve around a single legendary weapon or item of power. If your PCs are going to possess, interact with, and potentially use an object like this—it should have some personality. No matter what, it should provide you with plenty of options for compelling stories.

Assign priorities of 1 to 5 for the **reputation, attainability, complexity, potency,** and **appearance** of your legendary weapon without repeating a number.

Reputation

This determines what the world at large thinks of this weapon and the people who wield it. High priority brings accolades and expectations; low priority brings fear and dread.

1. Everyone speaks of this weapon with hushed reverence. No matter their relationship to the wielder, people will view anyone holding this weapon as a living myth.
2. Your allies see this weapon as a symbol of hope, and your enemies fear its power. Everyone sees the weapon as something more than the person wielding it.
3. The existence of this object is a secret or too complex for most people to understand. If the weapon gains a reputation, it will be as a result of the PC's actions.
4. This is a revered object, to the point that no one is considered worthy to hold it. Touching it may actually lower someone's opinion of you.
5. This weapon is the most loathed object in history. Everyone who has ever wielded it has used it to commit acts of unspeakable evil. Almost everyone will assume the worst of people holding this weapon.

Attainability

This determines how difficult it will be for the PCs to claim this object. It affects how much of your story will be about getting versus using a weapon.

1. This weapon was specifically entrusted to one of the PCs.
2. An ally to the PCs guards this weapon and is responsible for choosing who is worthy to hold it.
3. Anyone seeking to hold this weapon must go on a difficult and dangerous journey to claim it.
4. This weapon is already in the possession of one of the PCs' most dangerous enemies. They will need to take serious risks to claim it and prevent it from being used against themselves and their allies.
5. This weapon is cursed. It will seek out the PCs in order to bring power and ill fortune to them.

Complexity

This determines how easy a weapon is to use. Some are straight-forward; others have powers that elude understanding until critical moments. This will affect how quickly PCs or NPCs can use a weapon after they claim it.

1. This weapon offers not only power but also expertise, perhaps granting access to a portion of the knowledge and skill of those who have held it in the past.
2. Anyone who holds this weapon can control its power.
3. Only those the weapon deems worthy will be able to control its power.
4. The abilities of this weapon are only rumored or theoretical. Whoever seeks to control it will have to go through trials to unlock its secrets.
5. Using this weapon takes something significant from the user every time its powers are tapped. It leaves users almost irreparably changed.

Potency

This determines the overall capability of a weapon and defines how much it can shape the world. Some weapons are doomsday weapons; others depend on the user, or serve a narrow and specialized purpose.

1. This weapon possesses theoretically unlimited power. It could slay gods and reforge the foundations of the universe. With the right wielder there is no limit to what it could accomplish.
2. This weapon is unmatched by any other in terms of strength. It's an unstoppable force in battle, and when properly used the wielder will be nearly invincible.
3. This weapon possesses incredible potential, but its power is limited by the ability of its user.
4. This weapon is special compared to many, but applications of its power are limited.
5. This weapon's best days are behind it. The more it is used the less capable it becomes. A clever person could still put it to good use, but they must be strategic.

Appearance

This determines how recognizable a legendary weapon is as a significant object or weapon. This will dramatically affect your PC's ability to lay low, or convince others of the importance of their mission.

1. This weapon has an aura of divinity and nobility to it. Even unintelligent beasts would treat it with reverence and care.
2. This weapon looks almost aggressively mundane. There are no obvious features that would lead an untrained eye into believing that this weapon is as important as it is, making it perfect for heroes who wish to travel inconspicuously.
3. Even if it wasn't a weapon of mystical significance, it is crafted finely enough that it leads many to assume that whoever holds it must be important in some way. Used carefully it can open doors without its wielder having to do anything at all.

4. This weapon calls to people and demands to be noticed. Anyone who sees it will have at least a mild desire to hold it. Even if it is hidden away it will work to make itself known.
5. This weapon is terrifying to behold. Even those who come to wield it regularly are horrified by the process. Even if observers know the user well, they might still fear the worst.

Five Factions

A popular shortcut to conflict and intrigue is to create factions based on group motivations. This helps PCs anticipate consequences for their actions. It also provides you with opportunities to create dramatic tension between political powers. It's a little clichéd, but many clichés endure because they are useful.

For this exercise, we'll use prompts and rolls to create five distinct places, organizations, orders, and/or cultural backgrounds to quickly establish an identity for a region.

The Basics

 Roll d6 to determine the type of faction you're creating:

1. **State:** This culture is formed around a government. City-states often exist to provide protection, structure, and organization for the citizens living within them. Bonds between members are defined by political frameworks and civic structures.
2. **Family:** This culture is formed by a group of individuals bound by blood or marriage. Their views are dictated by elders and tradition. Bonds between members are clear even if emotionally fraught.
3. **Clan:** This culture blurs the line between many structures but especially that between family and state, creating affiliation by shared history and values. The bonds here are strongly tied to personal identity.

4. **School:** This culture is formed around an institution designed to study and instruct a particular subject or practice. Schools exist to collect and pass on knowledge, and some evaluate worth of members. Bonds surround teacher-student and colleague-to-colleague relationships.
5. **Company:** This culture is formed around a corporate entity. Companies provide resources and structure for members in hopes of creating profit. Bonds are based on hierarchical authority and function of position.
6. **Order:** This culture is formed around an organization dedicated to an ideology, like religion. Orders provide structure and resources to collectively pursue a common agenda. Bonds can be hierarchal, teacher-student, or colleague-to-colleague depending on the ethos of the order.

You'll also need to give your faction a treasure. This should have a thematic connection to what that faction loves most and might be an essential part of that activity.

 Choose or roll a d6 to create a treasure:

1. **A structure:** This is a building, monument, or city built by people.
2. **A place:** A stretch of land, natural formation, or established path created by forces beyond people.
3. **A text:** This might be a book, a story, or a secret that provides wisdom, knowledge, or power.
4. **A rarity:** This is something scarce or otherwise difficult to attain. It is a treasure most like what is typically thought of when hearing the word "treasure."
5. **A skill:** This is something members of a faction are capable of that outsiders are not. It might be powerful, useful, or just odd.
6. **A figure:** Someone living or dead who brings this faction pride, authority, or guidance.

Love of Strength

This faction defines itself through the celebration or even worship of strength. That strength can be physical, intellectual, emotional, spiritual, or magical. No matter how it manifests, the culture values power, minimizing vulnerability, and prioritizing achievement.

In a lot of fiction, cultures that value strength are cast as antagonists because of the connection between strength and aggression. While that's convenient for some stories, you don't necessarily need to move in that direction.

☀ **What does this faction love most about strength? Choose two:**

- ○ It provides safety.
- ○ It enables achievement.
- ○ It represents an ideal form.
- ○ It provides control.
- ○ It provides excitement.

How do people from this faction test and prove their strength?

What markers signify achievement or authority in this faction?

RELATIONSHIPS

✎ **Choose a faction that people who love strength respect or usually find an easy kinship with.**

Are these feelings the result of achievements by the other group, working relationships, or personality?

Does this dynamic have political implications?

✎ **Choose a faction that the people who love strength see themselves as vulnerable to or fear in some way.**

Are these feelings warranted?

How do the people who love strength defend themselves when around this faction?

Love of Knowledge

Members of this faction are dedicated to understanding some aspect of their world. This can manifest in the general study of all things or the specialization in a specific field of study like medicine, engineering, or magic. This culture values discovery, recording, and retention of knowledge.

✺ **What does this faction love most about knowledge? Choose two:**

- ○ It preserves the past.
- ○ It builds the future.
- ○ It satisfies curiosity.
- ○ It makes people useful.
- ○ It eases suffering.

How does this faction keep records of their knowledge? Where is it stored?

Does this faction share their knowledge? How do they decide who is worthy?

RELATIONSHIPS

✎ **Choose a faction that fascinates the people who value knowledge.**

Why do they wish to know more about this group?

To what lengths would they go to discover more?

✎ **Choose a faction that the people who value knowledge frequently work with.**

Who benefits most from this relationship?

In what situations do members of these groups most frequently interact?

Love of Communication

This faction is built around the complex art of communication. They can facilitate relations between houses, develop sophisticated forms of art and expression, or relish in gossip and espionage.

☀ **What does this faction love most about communication? Choose two:**

- ○ It creates beauty.
- ○ It creates peace.
- ○ It creates power.
- ○ It reveals truth.
- ○ It brings pleasure.

What form of communication originated with this faction and has spread to all the others?

What group or rank within this faction is respected by every other faction for their skill, power, or dangerousness?

Choose a faction that the people who love communication consider close allies.

How long have they held this alliance?

What would have to change for one of these parties to break this alliance?

Choose a faction that the people who love communication consider to be enemies.

How have the people who love communication acted against this faction, and do the leaders of this faction know?

What would have to change in order to reconcile this conflict?

Love of Nature

This faction is dedicated to acting as stewards and servants of natural forces. They might choose to live in a wild or hostile place, build culture around a close relationship with certain animals, or enact retribution when other factions harm the natural world.

✺ **What does this faction love most about nature? Choose two:**

- ○ It makes life possible.
- ○ It provides laws and stability.
- ○ It represents uncontested power.
- ○ It is a source of awe and wonder.
- ○ It rewards dedication and care.

How do the people who love nature live in a way that members of other factions could not?

What secret do they keep that eludes other factions?

RELATIONSHIPS

🖊 **Choose a faction that has struck an accord with the people who love nature.**

What does this agreement demand and what does it promise?

How has one of the parties involved come to resent this agreement?

🖊 **Choose a faction that borders the people who love nature.**

How do they benefit from this closeness?

What conflict do they take pains to avoid?

Love of Order

This faction is dedicated to upholding laws and respecting traditions. This might manifest as maintaining a justice system, leading a religion, or managing hierarchies. They prioritize laws and systems in all matters and only tolerate change when it follows a predetermined course.

✳ **What does this faction love most about order? Choose two:**

- ○ It exalts and values what is sacred.
- ○ It resolves disputes before they happen.
- ○ It gives purpose to what is chaotic.
- ○ It makes the world understandable and fair.
- ○ It connects people to their past.

What systems do the people who love order hold above all others?

What hypocrisies do they tolerate, if any?

RELATIONSHIPS

✏️ **Choose a faction that the people who love order consider superior (it can be themselves).**

How do they justify this claim?

What damage has this caused?

✏️ **Choose a faction that the people who love order tolerate reluctantly.**

What law prevents them from openly acting against this faction?

How does that faction test this dynamic?

Questover Country

Not every place in a world is a grand metropolis, legendary stronghold, or sacred ruin. However, even in small places there is magic and wonder.

Use the priority system to create an interesting place that might otherwise be lost and unappreciated. Assign priorities of 1 to 5 for the categories of **beauty**, **culture**, **amenities**, **wisdom**, and **secrets** without repeating a number.

Beauty

This can be natural or something made by people. Beauty isn't normally centered in RPGs, but diversions give you and the PCs a chance to explore and appreciate it.

1. This place offers singular beauty unmatched on the planet. If folks knew it existed they would flock here by the thousands to bask in its splendor.
2. There is surprising beauty here—humble, unassuming, but still remarkable. It is not rare but it is precious.
3. There is beauty here, but it mostly has to do with small things; a discerning poetic eye is needed to truly appreciate it.
4. This place is ugly, possibly because potential beauty has been twisted by imperfection or has fallen to decay.
5. This is the most offensively ugly place in the world. It's as if this is where the earth churns up all the profanity buried in the bowels of stone.

Culture

Even in small places people make art and celebrate life through creativity. Some places can surprise even the most worldly travelers with wonders that live in the heart of common folk.

1. This is a community that thrives with a unique and infectious creative spirit. Right now that spirit is on full, prominent display. Perhaps it is a festival, feast, or holy day. This will touch almost any soul in a profound way.

2. This is a community that cherishes something in a way that easily inspires joy. It's difficult for even the most jaded of travelers not to get swept up in the festivities.
3. Despite this community's small size, the people who live here find a way to connect and make an identity for their home. There is something unique here that stands out to everyone, even if they ultimately dismiss it.
4. Only in rare moments does the connection between people here reveal itself. Some will find this comforting as they project their own worldview onto this place; artistic souls will be unnerved and perhaps disturbed.
5. Culture here exists in hushed whispers that never reach the ears of an outsider. To almost all folk this place feels like a corpse—shaped like a living thing but with no heart or soul to make it move.

Amenities

Perhaps one of the most important qualities to a band of travelers is what a place can offer them for their stay. It could be a rundown backwater, or a hidden gem of hospitality.

1. This is a place of plenty and rarity. This place has everything the PCs need to be comfortable, and offers something truly unique that can't be found anywhere else.
2. For a community of its size, the amenities here are wondrous. They rival even the pleasures of a large metropolis. One or two PCs may even be able to find a luxury that normally eludes them.
3. This place meets the standard you need to make an acceptable stay. Perhaps the food is bland, the drink is weak, and the beds are cold, but there is enough here to get you the rest and supplies you need before moving on.
4. There is nothing here. PCs will have to scrape and search for any amenity they seek.
5. This place is actively hostile. Amenities are withheld from PCs or are somehow worse than nothing at all.

Wisdom

Sometimes you can only find clarity in places far removed from the places you imagine you are supposed to be. Other times a place can distract you from what you are meant to do and lead you astray.

1. There is a potentially life-changing lesson here and a guide to teach it. PCs can resolve their most haunting troubles if they wish and leave mentally and spiritually stronger than they arrived.
2. There is a lesson here that will challenge a PC's most dangerous assumptions. It will be difficult to process but the party will be better for it. They may leave feeling wounded, but they will heal stronger.
3. This place reinforces almost all of your PC's best assumptions. It underscores all the lessons your party has learned in the world outside. They will leave here feeling they are on the right path, although without having answered any critical questions.
4. This place is backward to a frustrating degree. The logic of the outside world does not apply here. Any effort to make sense of this place only leads to greater frustration. You will leave with nothing but anger and confusion.
5. There is a lesson here to challenge ideas that your party holds dear. It will be painful, and some may come away feeling as though they have lost something irreplaceable.

Secrets

Small places are ideal habitats for secrets because secrets live best in places where there are few souls to discover them. There is a reason heroes tend to come from places like this.

1. A myth is here rattling at the cage of the world. It is a secret that could change history. The PCs are destined to encounter it; the question is whether they will recognize it and how they will react to its discovery.

2. Somewhere in this sleepy place there is the key to a major scandal or a missing artifact critical to the world's history. It hides in plain sight and only careful eyes will be able to spot it.

3. There is some useful information here on a very small scale. The PCs will have to dig deep or be quite lucky in order to find it. It won't change the world, but it will be useful under the right circumstances.

4. There is nothing here. Places like this are small because no one goes here.

5. This place has no secrets, but it is hungry for them. It will work to pull truths out of the PCs. Each player should reveal something—potentially something dangerous or uncomfortable—about their character here. The danger that those secrets might one day be discovered now exists.

Sci-Fi

Like fantasy, science fiction is an extremely broad genre that covers a wide range of tones and subjects. Two sci-fi worlds can look almost completely different while still technically being in the same genre.

The core of sci-fi is speculative fiction: applying changes to the capabilities or conditions of human life and musing on what the consequences might be. Often this happens by introducing futuristic technology or investigating practical applications of theoretical concepts.

Our exercises in this chapter are focused mostly on space and far-future sci-fi because those subgenres are so popular for RPGs.

d20 Questions

Like fantasy, sci-fi has endless subgenres. Even if you already have one in mind, you will benefit from asking questions about what is possible and how that relates to familiar struggles.

 Roll a d20 and answer one question about your world for each person playing your game, including yourself:

1. How far have people made it into space?
2. What is the farthest natural boundary scientific exploration has pushed?
3. Are there humans in your world? If so, how focused is this story on their experiences?
4. *If this is in our future:* What struggles have followed us from now to then?

5. *If this is a different world:* What struggles might people from our world find familiar here?
6. What mysteries remain, despite scientific advancement?
7. What are the most common forms of transportation in this world?
8. How do communication tools in this world bring people closer together? In what ways do they drive people apart?
9. What do people in this world do for recreation?
10. What valuable things do powerful people invest their resources in acquiring?
11. Which historical events do people point to when trying to explain the world today?
12. What fears are common in this world?
13. What addictions exist in this world?
14. How have class systems evolved? Which people have access to necessary resources?
15. What natural laws no longer challenge people in this world?
16. Are there new forms of perception and sensory experience? What new phenomena are people able to observe or understand?
17. What object would most people in this world consider themselves totally lost without?
18. How has education changed? What are the most important skills for young people to learn?
19. What aspirations are common in this world that would be unthinkable in ours?
20. What's the farthest distance an ordinary person in this world can realistically hope to travel?

Time to Face the Strange

Time to Face the Strange is a solo or multiplayer minigame designed to quickly prompt you through creating revolutionary technology and deciding how it changes the world.

You'll need a deck of standard playing cards with jokers included. Shuffle the deck and arrange the cards facedown in a ring about a foot in diameter on a flat surface. It's fine if your ring is messy; that might even work to your advantage.

Innovation

Changing the world starts with innovation. Draw an Innovation card from the ring and reveal it to yourself and anyone else playing. The card's suit determines what field this technology advances. Its value determines the prompt you will use to create this innovation.

HEARTS: MEDICINE

This is an innovation in the field of medicine. That includes new medications, treatments, understanding of biology, and even potential modifications or enhancements for living beings.

DIAMONDS: TRANSPORTATION

This is an innovation that affects the process of moving people and things from one place to another. It can be new vehicles, changes to existing vehicles, new systems, or wholly new forms of transportation.

CLUBS: SECURITY

This is an innovation governing conflict, law enforcement, and surveillance. It can be a new weapon, technique for gathering data, or platform for hostility.

SPADES: COMMUNICATION

This is an innovation in the way people connect with one another. It can be a totally new device, a platform for interaction, a change to established communication technology, or a new way of communicating altogether.

	Medicine [Hearts]	Transportation [Diamonds]	Security [Clubs]	Communication [Spades]
A	A device that modifies the human experience permanently	A new publicly accessible mass transit solution	A weapon of mass destruction	A device that enables completely new types of communication

	Medicine [Hearts]	Transportation [Diamonds]	Security [Clubs]	Communication [Spades]
K	A device or treatment that enhances the capability of the human body	A vehicle or transportation system that makes it possible to visit previously unreachable places	A new standard for conflict that does not necessarily imply open warfare	A platform that offers a unique social experience
Q	A revolutionary way of understanding the body, mind, or genetics	A totally new transportation system or type of vehicle	A new military vehicle	A network that changes the way people interact
J	A treatment that changes the mortality rate for a common illness	A previously popular mode of transportation becomes almost completely obsolete	A new system of security or surveillance becomes a part of everyday life	Infrastructure that replaces an established system
10	A systemic change in how people access medical care	A new type of power or fuel for a popular type of transportation	An established form of weaponry becomes smaller or more portable	A new standard for transferring data or power

	Medicine [Hearts]	Transportation [Diamonds]	Security [Clubs]	Communication [Spades]
9	A new device capable of replacing vital systems in the body	A new innovation for efficiency in commercial transportation	A new nonlethal weapon	An essential device for modern communication
8	A device or system that makes monitoring and testing medical issues easier or more efficient	A novel passenger experience for commercial transportation	A new form of ammunition	A new way to carry or interact with an established style of communication
7	A new treatment that greatly extends the life span of almost any patient	An affordable consumer version of a heavily regulated or expensive vehicle	A type of military weaponry becomes less expensive and more available	A cheaper and more accessible version of a luxury technology
6	A generic affordable version of an essential medication or treatment	A new type of personal vehicle that is remarkably more versatile than existing options	A new type of personal firearm	A new format for home entertainment

	Medicine [Hearts]	Transportation [Diamonds]	Security [Clubs]	Communication [Spades]
5	A revolutionary change in corrective or assistive medical technology	A new network or infrastructure that drastically alters an established form of transportation	A new way to automate security or aggression	A new application developed for a common platform
4	A common treatment or test changes to incorporate more technology	A new method for transporting nonliving goods	A new type of surveillance equipment or surveillance network	A new program for news or entertainment
3	An established medication, treatment, test, or other medical tool becomes available without a prescription	A new professional application of an established piece of transportation technology	A new type of personal armor	A new small-scale system for data transfer

	Medicine [Hearts]	Transportation [Diamonds]	Security [Clubs]	Communication [Spades]
2	An established medical treatment or technology becomes a necessity for everyday life	A new material to integrate into an established mode of transportation	A new way to modify or distribute personal weaponry	A new solution for data storage
JR	A new disease, syndrome, or malady becomes a major threat to a large population	A scarce resource or new environmental condition makes a type of transportation completely impossible	A resource needed for a popular type of weaponry becomes scarce or depleted	A glitch, virus, or malware affects a common platform

Sometimes the most obvious answers are the best ones. Don't stress over creating something that seems revolutionary. It's hard to predict what will change the world.

For solo players we recommend drawing at least three innovations. Groups of three or four can give each player control over one innovation. Groups of five or more should work together on drawing and defining four innovations.

Changes

Now it's time to figure out how these innovations change the world. One at a time draw Change cards from the ring to pair with each innovation. The card's suit will determine what aspects of society it changes. Its value will determine what prompt you use to define that change.

HEARTS: SOCIAL

These are changes that affect how people interact, communicate, and relate to one another. That can mean adding or changing customs, interesting trends for expression, or upheaval and dramatic shifts in power structure.

DIAMONDS: ECONOMIC

These are changes that affect the economy. This can mean your innovation inspires an iconic trend, becomes the source of wealth for influential companies and figures, or initiates the birth or death of entire industries.

CLUBS: POLITICAL

These changes are tied to political powers and world events.

SPADES: PERSONAL

These changes impact an individual's experience of the world or themselves. Your innovation might introduce new daily annoyances, enable people to pursue new dreams, or drastically redefine the human experience.

	Social	Economic	Political	Personal
A	Inspires revolutionary upheaval, causing marginalized classes to seize rights, power, and prosperity	Helps create a boom of prosperity and economic mobility that benefits the majority of people	Brings about an unprecedented era of peace or aids a movement battling injustice and oppression	Redefines what it means to be human in a profound and permanent way
K	Causes the extinction of a popular social practice or institution	Creates a period of harsh economic depression	Causes the total collapse of a major world power	Directly or indirectly creates new life like AI or genetically engineered beings
Q	Introduces a new set of complex social conventions	Creates a new industry and bolsters existing ones	Uplifts a new or previously non-influential political power onto the world stage	Profoundly changes an individual's access to critical support systems
J	Creates a new religion or following that is dangerous in certain contexts	Becomes a major point of contention between influential powers	Becomes a major point of contention	Standardizes an enhanced quality of life

	Social	Economic	Political	Personal
10	Erodes trust and certainty in what used to be a valued cultural institution	Replaces the role of a previously prosperous and stable industry	Changes the legal landscape surrounding a major issue for decades	Changes the dynamic of interpersonal engagement for individuals with disabilities
9	Occasionally causes riots, demonstrations, or other forms of mass unrest	Becomes the focal point of labor organization, protests, or riots	Discredits or destroys an influential political leader	Ushers in a new widely accepted standard of personal liberty
8	Creates fervently opposed factions that enter into heated conflicts	Creates a new specialty profession	Helps a new political party form and mobilize	Creates a new form of self-expression
7	Creates a nearly insurmountable generational divide	Creates a stark divide between economic classes	Becomes the subject of heated disagreement between two influential political factions	Changes the basic path of the education system

	Social	Economic	Political	Personal
6	Imposes aspects of the culture of one nation on the rest of the world	Requires employers from just about every industry to change their structure	Directly or indirectly causes the death of a world leader	Creates a new standard for the experience of adulthood
5	Inspires new subculture identities	Causes a temporary bubble that bursts dramatically	Inspires a piece of legislation that dramatically changes the law in a major world power	Permanently or semipermanently reduces personal liberties for a large group of people
4	Creates new slang, language, or ways of understanding the world	Inspires a gold rush–esque competition to acquire specific resources	Becomes the focus of a major protest, violent conflict, or treaty negotiation	Creates a platform for people to explore and maintain a different sense of identity or self

	Social	Economic	Political	Personal
3	Inspires a movement of art, music, or performance	Helps a business or person rise to a position of significant cultural power	Causes a shift in the balance of interests who lobby or influence political leaders	Adds a host of new inconveniences to everyday life that people slowly come to accept
2	Defines the news cycle and cultural imagination for a period of time in a distinct way	Inspires an iconic marketing campaign that becomes a cultural reference point for a generation	Creates a scandal that defines a period in history or the career of a political figure	Takes the lives of many people, causing shared trauma for a generation
JR	Creates or refines a system of oppression	Actually doesn't exist in the way it was promised or causes a major unforeseen problem that forces the world to abandon it	Is completely ignored by powerful politicians despite affecting the lives of individuals dramatically	Forces society to confront one of the ugliest flaws in the human condition on a regular basis

Don't worry if you draw a prompt that doesn't seem to fit your innovation. Alexander Graham Bell probably didn't anticipate automated telemarketing scams when developing the telephone. The fun of this type of worldbuilding is discovering unintended consequences.

Allow the changes made by different innovations to interact and overlap with one another. Especially if you are playing in a group, work together to build on each other's ideas.

Don't be afraid to make big changes, like ending capitalism or phasing out the written word. Also don't be afraid to make small changes, like the proliferation of a catchy marketing jingle or the rise of an Internet celebrity.

Ending the Game

There are two ways to end *Time to Face the Strange*. The first is by drawing a set number of Change cards. You can choose to limit the number of Change cards based on how complicated and far-reaching you want the consequences of each innovation to be.

- Two or fewer innovations: four to five Change cards each
- Three to four innovations: three to four Change cards each
- More than five innovations: three Change cards each

The game also ends if you draw a card that breaks the ring of undrawn cards during the Change phase. Define this change the way you normally would, using the Change table. However, this change also directly or indirectly starts the **doomsday clock**. The value on that Change card determines how much time is left to avert an apocalyptic event, if any.

Doomsday Clock	
A	An obvious danger related to this change has made itself known early on. With hard work, crises can be averted before they start.
K	The current trajectory of events set in motion by this invention spells the end of life as we know it within a generation.
Q	There is an immediate world-ending threat posed by this invention or the changes it has wrought. Unless something is done the world will end within a year.
J	There is an immediate world-ending threat posed by this invention or the changes it has wrought. However, the timeline is unclear or too complicated to predict.
Even	The apocalypse can be averted only with immediate and decisive action. PCs have days to make a difference.
Odd	The changes caused by this development have created an urgent timeline to reduce the impact of an inevitable tragedy.
JR	The world is already too far gone to save, and its inevitable collapse has been concealed by powerful interests.

How Far How Fast

Interstellar travel is a mainstay of many sci-fi settings. It allows intelligent species to visit strange planets and connect with life-forms beyond their imagination. How that travel works can have a huge impact on the setting's tone and the scenarios players encounter.

Use the priority system to define interstellar travel. Assign priorities of 1 to 5 for **distance**, **speed**, **costs**, **safety**, and **scale** without repeating a number.

Distance

The standard distance for space travel determines the stage for stories in your world. Settings that stay within the confines of a single solar system limit options and force PCs into tough choices about known quantities. Interstellar distance forces PCs to balance many cultural personalities and allows them space to hide and fade into a crowd. Intergalactic distance makes travel unpredictable and full of discovery.

1. It is possible to travel beyond the boundaries of the visible universe. As the universe expands, space travel expands with it, allowing characters in this setting to go anywhere their imaginations can take them.
2. Space travel is intergalactic and can take characters anywhere within the visible universe. The near-infinite clusters of far-off galaxies are open for observation and exploration.
3. Space travel is limited to anywhere within an individual galaxy. This opens up countless stars, planets, and cosmic objects. However, traveling beyond the borders of a galaxy is still only theoretical and experimental.
4. Space travel is limited to only the nearest stars. While it is possible to go just about anywhere within a solar system, traveling more than a few light years is beyond reach.
5. Space travel only takes place within a solar system. Anything involving even a nearby star would take a special experimental journey.

Speed

The speed of space travel determines how intrusive travel is for PCs and the stress they carry from one location to the next. An instantaneous journey means travel doesn't really get in the way, but there is no downtime between locations. A journey of a few days to years makes the decision to travel to a new location a much larger consideration, but also means there is time for characters to process events between locations.

1. Travel is instantaneous, taking no time at all. Perhaps ships and people are able to move at several times the speed of light, or two different points in space-time can be connected. Either way, not much happens during a journey.
2. Travel is limited only by the time it takes to charge an engine or plot a course. Whatever interstellar process vessels use, the trip happens in seconds—but getting ready for that jump can take hours or even days depending on the circumstances.
3. The time it takes to travel a distance of light years is greatly reduced. A trip over an unthinkably vast distance might take just a few weeks, days, or even hours.
4. If travel is faster than light at all, it is only barely. Depending on how far people are traveling, a voyage can take weeks, months, or even years. There might be solutions that allow travelers to travel in stasis, but it takes a very long time to reach far distances.
5. Travelers and vessels cannot move faster than light. Any journey between stars takes years, and even travel within solar systems could take weeks or months.

Costs

The cost of space travel determines how much narrative space that travel takes up when PCs aren't currently making a trip. Low-cost settings only slow PCs when there is serious trouble with their equipment. Toward the middle range of costs, PCs need to think about where they are going to acquire fuel or the funds every time they travel—which means cost will play a role in most stories. For high-cost settings every single trip becomes a major decision for the group.

1. There is no cost for interstellar travel. Whatever system characters have devised for travel does not consume energy, fuel, or resources of any kind. There might still be challenges involved, but they are purely logistical.
2. Travel does have a cost, but it only needs energy or fuel sources that are generally plentiful and renewable. The only circumstances where characters might have to worry are ones where they are contending with damage or external challenges.
3. The resources needed to travel between stars are generally available but create a consistent cost for the travelers. Perhaps fuel and energy are commercially available but expensive—or it takes time to gather and synthesize the proper resources. Either way, getting ready to travel is a regular chore.
4. Space travel depends on rare or expensive forms of energy or fuel. Long-distance travel is mostly limited to governments, guilds, and corporations with vast resources. Anyone operating outside these systems has to steal or prospect in order to travel a long distance.
5. In order to go long distances, travelers have to sacrifice something unique and precious. This could be the lives of thinking creatures, consuming energy from planets or stars, or even metaphysical costs like souls. Either way, the resources needed to travel are devastating and cause many to wonder whether the cost is worth it.

Safety

Safety determines how much action intersects with travel. In high-safety settings, there is very little risk of damaging equipment or attracting unwanted attention when initiating a jump. In medium-safety settings, travel can get you into and out of trouble frequently, and it isn't uncommon to jump out of a frying pan and into a fire. In low-safety settings, every jump is a high-risk move that nearly guarantees a fight, a desperate flurry of repairs, or a funeral.

1. There is never a question of safety for space travel. All systems are so thoroughly tested, regulated, and engineered that they automatically activate fail-safes in every conceivable dangerous situation. You are safer traveling through space than you would be at many of the locations you could visit.

2. In the vast majority of circumstances there is little risk involved in space travel. If systems are damaged or conditions in space are extraordinarily volatile, that risk grows. Otherwise the PCs contend with the known dangers of their destinations.

3. There are risks in space travel, but they are mitigated by calculation, preparation, and procedure. In most cases it is safe to travel in space as long as you have the time and energy to follow those procedures. Even with careful planning, enemies might still appear to cause complications.

4. Space travel is always a bit dicey. While it is possible to travel safely, it depends on optimal conditions. Unless you are following established routes with the best information available, you risk damage or even total destruction. Beings like pirates, monsters, and other hostile powers potentially represent a threat.

5. Space travel is never safe. Something about the engines that make long-distance travel possible is always volatile. Perhaps the amount of energy required to move over great distances always risks meltdown, crew stasis has a high mortality rate, or jumping from place to place requires moving through hell dimensions. No matter what, traveling a long way has a good chance of getting travelers killed or worse.

Scale

The scale of space travel determines the mobility of your PCs and the universe around them. In large-scale worlds massive objects the size of stars have the ability to hop around the universe—making a sense of place very abstract. Toward the middle range you choose whether interstellar ships must be smaller or whether they are dependent on larger vessels and stations to move around. At the lowest scales PCs might have to travel as squads of individual ships, or deal with the fact that high-speed long-distance travel isn't really a possibility at all.

1. Far-space travel can accommodate ships and stations of enormous size, moving objects the size of suns and small solar systems. The limitations of transportation are almost entirely based on the limitations of engineering. If you can build it, you can move it.
2. Long-distance travel methods can accommodate ships the size of nations or moons. Nearly entire civilizations can cross the stars on massive vessels that mimic the space and comfort of terrestrial life.
3. There are two possibilities:
   1. Long-distance travel methods can only accommodate ships the size of buildings and smaller, at most moving around a few thousand crew members at once.
   2. Long-distance travel methods depend on vessels or stations the size of cities to work properly. It is almost impossible for smaller vessels to move over great distances alone.
4. Far-space travel can only accommodate small vessels with a handful of travelers or maybe only single pilots. Whatever technology enables this travel does not scale up very well.
5. The fastest and farthest travel methods can't carry thinking creatures at all. Most likely they can't even move objects. However, they do allow messages to be sent between stars and across the universe. People separated by light years can still communicate in real time.

It's McGuffium

Many sci-fi stories revolve around the pursuit of rare and powerful substances that make technological wonders possible. Substances like this are an extremely convenient storytelling tool because they justify action and conflict. They also provide explanations for normally impossible sci-fi tech. The impossible is possible because of these plot enablers, sometimes known as "McGuffium," and that's what makes them so desirable. (The word "MacGuffin" was first used by Alfred Hitchcock in his films to refer to something that has no purpose other than to drive the plot.)

This exercise will help you develop a coveted miraculous substance for your own world that will keep thrusters burning and blasters firing session after session.

Properties

One of the most fun things about MacGuffin substances is the marvelous properties they possess. Even if the MacGuffin is miraculous, not all of its properties are beneficial, and that's also part of the fun!

For every **beneficial** property you select for this plot device, choose one **dangerous** property and one **curious** property:

Beneficial	Dangerous	Curious
Creates a reaction that gives off nearly infinite stable energy	Is toxic when handled in unshielded environments	Constantly changes shape
Has an atomic signature that can be found in multiple dimensions	Extremely volatile and capable of damaging entire solar systems	Never appears to be the same color to different observers
Absorbs energy efficiently and reliably	Extremely dense and heavy in a natural state	Shifts properties as long as it is not being observed

Beneficial	Dangerous	Curious
Creates reaction that opens wormholes	Unstable in natural conditions, it can disappear or destruct if not handled with care	Has an inverse relationship between mass and weight
Allows the manipulation of gravity	Randomly creates wormholes or dimensional breaches	Extremely bouncy
Allows travel through time	Causes hallucinations and personality changes in living beings who come in contact with it	Glows in the dark
Grants supernatural abilities to beings who come in contact with it	Gives living beings false memories	Makes an eerie sound
Is nearly indestructible	Attracts extradimensional predators	Is in certain conditions invisible
Transforms toxic matter into usable elements	Corrupts the natural growth of life-forms	Is extremely brittle but self-heals
Enables stasis for living beings	Degrades equipment around it at an extremely accelerated rate	Is not made of atoms
Is essential for producing advanced processors	Reacts negatively with itself in large amounts	Is not affected by a major force like gravity

Beneficial	Dangerous	Curious
Has boundless destructive potential	Damages artificial intelligence it comes into contact with	Tastes like root beer
Enables shielding technology	Requires constant monitoring across multiple sensor arrays	Has a surface that reflects objects but not people
Extends the natural life span of living beings	Has an actively malicious intelligence	Does not reflect sound or light
Creates entrances and exits to hyperspace lanes	Only gives reading to sensors on a delay	Always comes in paired deposits

Select as many properties as you like; just be aware that a greater number of properties makes things more complicated.

Location

One of the most important things about MacGuffins is that they are difficult to get. To create a compellingly challenging new location for your MacGuffin, ask the following questions:

☀ **Are the PCs already in great danger?**
    O Yes   O No

☀ **Are they undersupplied?**
    O Yes   O No

☀ **Are they out of other options?**
    O Yes   O No

Roll two d6 and add 1 for every question you answered with "yes."

1. **On a result of 10 or higher**, the PCs should choose one of the following to find a source of McGuffium:
   - The source provides just barely enough McGuffium to suit PC needs; choose one danger from the following list.
   - The source is plentiful; choose two dangers from the list.

2. **On a result of 7–9**, the PCs manage to find a substantial source of McGuffium, but they will have to pay a steep cost to go after it. Choose one cost:
   - Make a promise to a dangerous person or faction.
   - Put an ally in harm's way.
   - Damage a critical piece of equipment.
   - Threaten to compromise a moral principle.

3. **On a result of 6 or less**, the PCs manage to find a huge supply of MacGuffins; select three dangers.

DANGERS
- The source is extremely far away, and it will take a great deal of time and resources to reach it.
- Space surrounding the source is hazardous with nebula, ion storms, asteroids, or black holes.
- Atmosphere or terrestrial conditions surrounding the source are dangerous.
- There is an aggressive bestial life-form making a home near the source.
- The source is deep inside hostile territory, and discovery within those borders would be disastrous.
- The McGuffium is already in the possession of one of the PC's most dangerous enemies.
- It is easy to get to where the McGuffium is, but almost impossible to get back.

Name

Finally, you need to give your McGuffium a fittingly sci-fi–sounding name. If you're having trouble thinking of one, draw two cards from a standard deck of playing cards (jokers included) and compare them to the chart here to generate a name:

	First Half	Second Half
A	Void/Dark/Abyss/Abyssal-	[Insert random number]
K	[Name of an ancient god]-	[Name referencing a famous physicist]
Q	[Name referencing a famous physicist]-	[Insert existing element] [Insert existing element] -alloy
J	[Insert planet name]	[Insert existing element]
10	Infini-/Fractal-/Fract-	anthium
9	Cos-/Cosme-/Cosmi-	plex
8	Stella-/Stellar-	teline
7	Techno-/Tech-/Techni-	lar
6	Celest-/Celestial-	ridium
5	Nuk-	ilium
4	Duri-	anium
3	Electri-	steel
2	Quanti-	metal
JR	Element-/[Insert random letter or number]	[Name referencing a corporation in your setting]

Void Warper's Local 301

In sci-fi stories people live alongside intelligent robots, terraform inhospitable planets, and broker peace with alien worlds. It's easy to forget that someone builds those robots, services the terraforming machines, and cleans up after the interplanetary negotiations. This exercise will help you ground your sci-fi world by developing a union to manage the labor that makes all of the wonders of tomorrow possible.

◉ Why a Union?

Sci-fi tends to lean heavily on federations, governments, religions, militaries, and corporations as influential organizations. Most of these organizations concern themselves with big ideas and lofty goals. Unions represent working people trying to make their lives a little better. Adding a perspective like that grounds your setting and opens the door for interesting conflict.

Industry

First you'll need to decide exactly what kind of workers your union represents. Start by naming a core concept in your world. It should be something that you think really defines your setting as sci-fi. Try to sum it up in a few words like "interstellar travel," "full-dive VR," or "robot boyfriends."

CORE CONCEPT

While this concept is definitely made possible by dazzling futuristic science, it's also made possible by people. Somewhere there are beings mining the fuel for spaceships, maintaining the servers for the matrix, and assembling robot boyfriends.

 Roll a d12 to determine an industry that supports your concept:

1. **Construction:** Labor for the creation of large-scale projects like buildings, large spaceships, space stations, and infrastructure.
2. **Transportation:** Operation of public and private transit.

3. **Manufacturing:** Creation of all medium and small goods. These can be consumer goods or equipment for industry and government.
4. **Agriculture:** The production of plant- and animal-based goods. This can also be terraforming and maintaining environments.
5. **Service:** Workers responsible for person-to-person interactions and managing client experiences.
6. **Maintenance:** The technical upkeep of vehicles, buildings, and infrastructure. This also covers cleaning and waste disposal.
7. **Programming:** The creation and maintenance of digital programs and platforms.
8. **Mining:** The large-scale harvesting of nonliving resources.
9. **Education:** Teaching at any level.
10. **Engineering:** The design of goods, vehicles, buildings, and infrastructure.
11. **Medical:** Any profession related to health, wellness, and medicine.
12. **Media:** The production of information and entertainment products. This covers journalism, writing, acting, and all broadcast-related professions.

Think about how that industry supports your concept. Especially if things don't seem like a match initially, consider what needs to be in place for things to run smoothly or what people need to do when things go wrong. Then answer this question:

How is this job essential?

Everyday Weirdness

Part of the fun in grounding sci-fi with real-world institutions is the juxtaposition between the ordinary and extraordinary. A factory that produces spaceship parts is way more fun if workers need jet pack certifications or have safety guidelines to avoid time paradoxes. Use the following questions to create a strange futuristic workplace:

🖊 **How do workers use this sci-fi concept every day as a tool?**

🖊 **What sci-fi concept is a common worksite hazard?**

🖊 **What sci-fi concept is part of essential safety equipment?**

🖊 **What sci-fi concept is considered one of the best parts of the job?**

Composition

In the real world humans have trouble getting along; in sci-fi things can be even more complex because humans might work alongside other intelligent beings. Nonhuman union members have different needs and perspectives. That can serve as a source of internal tension or just make your creation feel more unique.

☀ **Choose one of the following potential sci-fi worker categories:**

- ○ **Human:** An average person from the planet Earth, like the people you live around today.
- ○ **Transhuman:** A human who has been altered by scientific advancement to the point they look different or experience the world differently. Examples include a cyborg, a genetically engineered person, or a psychic.
- ○ **AI:** Artificial intelligence that is self-aware enough to act and feel like an individual. These can be robots, androids, or programs on a computer.
- ○ **Terran:** A human born on a planet other than Earth. This could be a place in our solar system, a distant star, or even a space station. "Terran A–D" denote Terrans from different points of origin that might not see eye to eye.
- ○ **Alien A:** These are aliens who are extremely similar to humans in appearance and ability.
- ○ **Alien B:** These aliens have some similarities to humans but at least one dramatic difference like colorful skin, extra limbs, unusual senses, and superhuman abilities.
- ○ **Alien C:** Aliens who look and act dramatically different than humans and are more similar to non-mammalian life-forms. They probably can't communicate the way humans are used to.
- ○ **Alien D:** Aliens that are almost incomprehensibly different than humans. They probably have more in common with insects, slime molds, or microscopic organisms.

Consult the top row of this chart to find the subgenre that best describes your setting and roll a d10 five times to determine the composition of workers in your union:

	Near Future	Far Future	Space	Deep Space	Intergalactic/ Denominational
1	Human	Human	Human	Human	Human
2	Human	Human	Trans-human	Human/ Terran B	Human/Terran
3	Human	Trans-human	Terran A	Human/ Terran B	Human/Terran
4	Human	Trans-human	Terran B	Terran	AI
5	Trans-human	Trans-human	Terran C	AI	Alien A
6	Trans-human	AI	AI	Alien A	Alien B
7	Trans-human	AI	Alien A	Alien B	Alien C
8	AI	AI	Alien A	Alien B	Alien C
9	AI	Terran	Alien B	Alien C	Alien D
10	AI	Terran	Alien B	Alien C	Alien D

Each roll represents a roughly even share of population within the union. If a category or result comes up more than once, it simply has a larger population and more influence within the union.

Status

Unions are established to represent and advocate for their workers. However, even successful unions struggle with corruption. No matter what challenges they face, unions are always interesting forces in the world of industry, politics, and crime.

First answer the following questions about your union:

✳ **Has this union already won at least one critical battle?**
O Yes   O No

✳ **Are union leaders considered powerful?**
O Yes   O No

✳ **Do members have something to lose?**
O Yes   O No

[6] **Roll two d6 and add 1 for every question you answered with "yes."**

Based on the results, choose a status that fits your vision for your union. The table later in the chapter provides choices for **strengths, demands, corruptions,** or **threats**.

1. **On a result of 6 or lower, the union is either new:**
    O Members have just started to organize after being pushed to a breaking point by ownership.
    O Choose two strengths, two demands, and three threats.

    Or struggling:
    O The union exists but faces substantial opposition and has begun to deteriorate under pressure.
    O Choose one strength, one corruption, two demands, and two threats.

2. **On a result of 7–9, the union is either established:**
   ○ The union has grown strong enough to tackle difficult issues, but their fight is not over. They struggle to maintain momentum after reaching certain goals.
   ○ Choose two strengths, one demand, two corruptions, and one threat.

   Or battling:
   ○ The union is strong, but so are their adversaries. As the conflict escalates, outside forces seek to exploit their power.
   ○ Choose three strengths, two demands, one corruption, and three threats.

3. **On a result of 10 or higher, a union is either languishing:**
   ○ This union's most important battles are behind it. They still hold power, but a weaker ideology means it is not always used effectively. Despite this they still serve some essential functions.
   ○ Choose two strengths, one demand, two corruptions, and one threat.

   Or co-opted:
   ○ This union no longer represents the interests of its members, if it ever did in the first place. It levies collective power to serve criminal or ruling class interests, forcing members to be compliant.
   ○ Choose two strengths and three corruptions.

Strengths	Demands	Corruptions	Threats
Members are loyal to one another	Better pay	The union favors nepotism over need	The owners are wealthy and influential
Workers have valuable experience and expertise	Safer working conditions	Leadership serves an external interest	The public is not sympathetic
The union has resources to support vulnerable members	Better tools	Membership has been infiltrated by an external interest	A significant number of workers haven't joined
The union has a good reputation with the public	Expanded benefits	Union resources are not used appropriately	The economy makes unemployment risky
The union is very large	Manageable hours	Not all members are represented fairly	There are potential scabs
The union has clever leaders	Societal support and protection for members	Leaders have made questionable alliances	There is distrust between certain member groups

Five Fighters

In many stories spaceships are a means to an end. You want to explore space and you need a tool to make that possible. However, they are also an opportunity to add personality and mythology to your setting. This exercise will help you develop five unique star fighters for your setting.

Choose from the lists of thematic and stylistic rules for five different classes of star fighter and use them to design distinct ships for your setting!

The Underdog's Teeth

When flying into battle against evil empires, heroes need something that makes them a credible threat. This fighter is the iconic symbol of resistance and gives freedom fighters the edge they need to win.

☀ **Choose two advantages:**

- ○ It's faster than most fighters.
- ○ It's tougher than most fighters.
- ○ It's got more firepower than most fighters.
- ○ It's easy to disguise.
- ○ It can warp, jump, go FTL easily.

☀ **Choose two drawbacks:**

- ○ It requires a base or capital ship to launch from.
- ○ It won't operate in atmosphere.
- ○ It's expensive to replace.
- ○ Maintenance issues are common.
- ○ It takes more than one being to operate.

CREATE A LOOK

Choose one from each of the categories (color, style, and weathering):

☀ Color

- **Bright colors:** These ships have a bright, friendly palette that stands out.
- **Reserved colors:** These fighters have colorful strategic highlights that make them stand out but don't overpower the design.
- **Individualistic colors:** Pilots and crews decorate ships, and the fleet is not cohesive.

☀ Style

- **Aerodynamic frame:** This ship is based on an existing airplane design.
- **Apex frame:** This ship is reminiscent of a powerful winged predator.
- **Dart frame:** This ship is long and pointy.
- **Dynamic frame:** Parts move or shift to contextually change the silhouette of this fighter.

☀ Weathering

- **Scarred:** Most ships are covered in scratches and burns from frequent battles.
- **Cobbled:** Most ships were built out of salvage. Seams show; lines are mismatched.
- **Ancient:** Rust, stains, and patches are common in nonvital areas.

The Face of Oppression

For antagonists, you need something that inspires fear, so your heroes can show courage when they rise up. These are the enforcers emblematic of a fascist empire or growing militaristic threat.

☀ **Choose two threats:**

- ○ They are always deployed in large numbers.
- ○ They pursue orders until destroyed.
- ○ They are always equipped to attack non-combat targets.
- ○ Their presence means a command ship is never far away.
- ○ Squads are networked; getting spotted by one means getting targeted by them all.

☀ **Choose two harshnesses:**

- ○ There are no shields to protect them.
- ○ They make a terrible sound.
- ○ They are drones.
- ○ Their primary weapons are visually distinct.
- ○ All ships are new because they never bother to salvage or repair.

CREATE A LOOK

There is something in the design of these ships that signals a human or animal part and evokes a primal fear:

☀ **Choose one option in each of the following categories:**

- ○ **Eyes:** Windows, weapons, and other components make this fighter look as though it has one or more unblinking eyes.
- ○ **Teeth:** Something about the frame of the ship evokes a maw full of jagged teeth.
- ○ **Skulls:** The frame is based on a human or animal skull.
- ○ **Horns:** There are sharp gnarling protrusions based on antlers or horns.

☀ Choose an architectural style:

- ○ **Sharp:** The lines on this ship are expressed like jutting thorns or blades.
- ○ **Geometric:** The shape of the ship is broken into blocky angles. Anything that would be round has lines and edges.
- ○ **Brutalist:** Stark minimalism in frame. They are shapes with as little design as possible.
- ○ **Alien:** This design works very hard to look like a thing no human would imagine. A trypophobic succulent made of dark steel.

☀ Choose a color scheme:

- ○ Black and white
- ○ Black and red
- ○ Black, white, and red
- ○ Black and neon, like a poison jungle frog

VARIANTS

Evil empires don't value creativity. Bombers and fighters are slight variations of their basic ship.

☀ Choose one of the following:

- ○ It's like they glued two basic fighters together.
- ○ It's just bigger.
- ○ It has a fin now.

Slow, Ugly, and Critical

Rebel fleets have to make do with what they can find. That is almost never good. This fighter is outdated, ugly, and absolutely essential to victory. They need to be escorted everywhere they go, and if you leave them behind all you can do is retreat.

Every vessel of this type can carry enough firepower to sink a capital ship.

✴ **Choose one additional signature advantage:**

- ○ The design is based on a civilian cargo ship, making it easy to train pilots.
- ○ It is infinitely repairable and functions on scrap parts.
- ○ Resembles non-combat vessels, making it easy to hide in ports.

✴ **Choose two flaws:**

- ○ These ships are protected only by armored hulls, making them vulnerable to attack.
- ○ These ships are among the slowest and least maneuverable vessels in service.
- ○ You only get one shot with their payload.
- ○ They can't be stealthy.
- ○ They carry almost no defensive weapons.

To create a look, choose one from each category (style and color):

✴ **Style**

- ○ **Utilitarian:** Based on a cargo vessel like a truck, van, or cargo ship. Big, bulky, and boring.
- ○ **Just an "x" with thrusters:** Look for the most boring object in your room. That is the basis for the silhouette of this ship.
- ○ **Font:** Pick a letter or symbol from your keyboard. The frame of this ship is based on that.

☀ Color

- ○ **Patchy:** Every single ship looks as though it has been built out of progressively older versions of the same ship. The hulls are a patchwork of grays accented by rust.
- ○ **Simple:** These ships get damaged so often there is no sense in wasting good paint on them. They are usually sprayed down with the cheapest color available.
- ○ **Scarification:** The color of these ships is always bare metal, but engineering crews weld art onto the hulls. They don't look like much from far away, but if you get close you can tell someone loves it.

The Secret Weapon

Some missions are so important you need to take a risk by deploying the ship that's rare, expensive, and does what all the others can't.

☀ Choose two advantages:

- ○ Its conventional arms can pierce any shield.
- ○ It's unquestionably the fastest fighter around.
- ○ It can carry a devastating weapon.
- ○ Its maneuverability is unmatched.
- ○ It can physically engage enemy ships.

☀ Choose two signature flaws:

- ○ It can only be flown by highly trained pilots.
- ○ There are only a dozen prototypes in existence.
- ○ It requires a rare and expensive type of fuel.
- ○ It lacks the ability to jump, warp, or go FTL, so it requires a capital escort.
- ○ It can only fly for a limited time before it needs a charge or tow.

To create a look, choose one from each category (style and color):

✳ Style

- ○ **Asymmetric:** This ship's frame is unbalanced. It wouldn't be aerodynamic in atmosphere, but it looks cool in space.
- ○ **Mobile:** The frame of this ship is always moving somehow. Rotating, transforming, and flaring. This ship constantly reassembles itself to fulfill different functions.
- ○ **Anthropomorphic/Animalistic:** The design is based on a recognizable human or animal frame.

✳ Color

- ○ Gold, silver, and chrome
- ○ Crystalline or prismatic
- ○ Stealth black with fleet racing stripe

The Shadow

Fascist empires tend to define themselves by creating a sense of uniformity that drowns individuality. However, they also love hierarchy, and it's useful to have a ship that can elevate conflicts without making them hopeless. The Shadow represents the looming threat of imperial power in a visually compelling way. It exists to menace heroes through strength and subtlety.

✳ Choose two threats:

- ○ These ships are equipped for stealth.
- ○ These ships are equipped with drones that can spy or scramble radar.
- ○ These ships have powerful conventional arms that cut through shields.
- ○ A single ship can outmaneuver a full squad of traditional fighters.
- ○ Pilots for these ships are the result of an elite conditioning and modification program.

✳️ **Choose an intended function for these fighters:**

- ◯ Intelligence gathering
- ◯ Command escort
- ◯ Target assassination

To create a look, choose one from each category (style, lighting, and color):

✳️ **Style**

- ◯ **Enhanced standard model:** It looks like an extra-fancy version of most imperial fighters.
- ◯ **Dark mirror:** It looks like a twisted version of a rebellion fighter, informed by the stylistic quality you chose for the Face of Oppression.
- ◯ **Minimalist:** It's an unassuming simple shape made to be understated and menacing.

✳️ **Lighting**

- ◯ **Battle mode:** When this ship engages in a dogfight its silhouette changes and its weaponry becomes more visible, glowing a bloody crimson, sickly green, or violet.
- ◯ **Streaking path:** When engaged in complex maneuvers this ship leaves a ghostly trail of engine light.
- ◯ **Inhuman glare:** The cockpit is lit in a way that evokes a wrathful or impassive stare.

✳️ **Color**

- ◯ Bright crimson
- ◯ Obsidian
- ◯ Only visible in the silhouette of flames and blaster fire

Horror

Horror investigates fear and suspense through macabre imagery and tense scenarios. Unless it is blended with another genre, it usually takes place in a modern or familiar setting.

This kind of setting presents two problems. The first is limitations. Modern and other real-world settings don't let you paint with a broad brush in the way wholly invented settings do. It's tough to make up stuff for Chicago, because it already exists.

The second problem with these settings is experience. Nobody knows what you're supposed to do on a spaceship or in a magical castle, but we've all been taught how to react when things go wrong in our homes. One of the most important jobs in creating a horror story is isolating players from solutions that push their problems away from their characters.

These exercises are designed to help you create within those confines. There are plenty of opportunities for small-scale worldbuilding that fit in familiar contexts. We also have some solutions for making places that cut the PCs off from easy answers.

Finally, everything is designed to help create a creepy atmosphere that keeps the threats in your world dangerous and out of sight until the final act.

d20 Questions

 Roll a d20 for each player in the game (including yourself) and answer the question:

1. How is the place where this story is set isolated from the outside world?
2. When victims look for people who have been in similar situations, what do they find?
3. If there are other people around, what reason do they have to distrust the PCs?
4. How is the environment uniquely dangerous, outside the main threat of horror?
5. What in this environment forces at least one of the PCs to confront a tragedy from their past?
6. What forces outside the PCs' control bind them to this place?
7. What warnings do the PCs need to ignore in order to put themselves in danger?
8. Who apart from the PCs understands the horror? How has this knowledge harmed them?
9. Where can the PCs go to find potentially lifesaving information? How is it incomplete?
10. What about this place creates feelings of shame in one of the PCs?
11. How is the horror personally tied to at least one of the PCs?
12. What is the most undeniably beautiful thing about this place?
13. What mundane obstacle exists here to frustrate the PCs when they try to take simple precautions?
14. Why would well-meaning people take steps to conceal vital information?
15. What valuable thing here could compel people to take risks?
16. What is the most secure place here and how is that security fragile?
17. Where could a person get lost here?
18. Who supports or worships the horror here?
19. What is the worst consequence of the horror fulfilling its agenda?
20. What powerful benevolent force seems present but somehow inactive or out of reach?

Anatomy of a Monster

There are plenty of great examples of effective monsters in pop culture. It's easy to draw on tropes and come up with something that works. With a little effort though, you can take things further.

Monsters are physical manifestations of theme. They make statements about the nature of fear and how your story addresses it. There are lots of ways to understand fear, but we'll look at monsters in terms of their relationship with **the unknown** and **the familiar**.

Horror—especially in games—depends on the audience identifying with feelings of powerlessness. Monsters in form, behavior, and function work by controlling the audience's access to knowledge to create feelings of unease. All monsters exploit our relationship with the things we know to put us in situations where we confront the things we don't know.

Picture a person holding a knife. The less an audience knows about this person, the more monstrous they become. Imagine this person standing in a kitchen versus standing silhouetted in a door. Taking away identifiable context and physical features raises questions: *Who is this? Why do they have a knife? Do they mean me harm?* That gives the audience an opportunity to fill in the gaps with fear.

This also works if you remove this person's features in other ways (putting them in a mask, for example). You can make things even scarier by presenting a scenario where someone with a knife is in the room but they can't be seen *at all*. The one thing the audience knows is that there is danger, and so their minds create a monster.

With that knowledge, let's make a cool horror monster by defining its **nature**, **appearance**, **violence**, and **vulnerabilities**.

Nature

A monster's nature defines their behavior; it explains why they do terrible things and what fears define them. Because the root of monstrosity is fear given form, there are too many sources to define in a single exercise, chapter, or even book. Instead, we broke down the roots of a monster's nature into four basic categories: **human**, **bestial**, **supernatural**, and **alien**.

HUMAN

A "human" monstrous nature is driven by fears of human thought and capability. A violent murderer, a vengeful ghost, and a conquering invader are all demonstrating aspects of a human nature. Those actions are a terrible potential we recognize in ourselves.

Our familiarity with human behavior makes it terrifying. Giving a monster a shade of humanity links it to the darkest parts of our nature. Your PCs all understand that on some level.

BESTIAL

A monster with a bestial nature is based on primal fears of dangerous creatures. A vicious wolf baring its teeth, a lurking venomous snake, and a powerful charging bull are shades of bestial nature. Bestial fears work by making people feel small, vulnerable, and helpless. Once again, this nature plays on what we *know* to be dangerous, but it's a more external representation of our fears.

A bestial monster emphasizes the uncontrollable qualities of living things. They are capable of terrible violence, but are devoid of intentional malice or cruelty. The dispassionate certainty of instinct is chilling in a much different way than the intentional violence of a human nature.

SUPERNATURAL

A supernatural nature is based around systems rather than beings. An incurable disease, a terrible curse, and the unknowable nature of death contain shades of the supernatural. Monsters with this kind of nature are the most firmly related to understandable systems—rules and laws. These are forces we understand but can't control or predict.

A monster with a supernatural nature projects inevitability. They present danger that cannot be reasoned with or turned aside. If PCs understand the rules and systems that govern a monster's behavior and danger, they will know when they are at risk. That is a powerful tool for creating the right atmosphere.

ALIEN

An alien nature is based around concepts humans struggle to identify with or even understand. Strange life-forms, foreign thought processes, and challenging concepts like chaos are part of an alien nature. Alien monsters present frightening images without any comforting connective tissue to help us understand them.

A monster with an alien nature defies explanation even as it reveals itself. This is a really tricky nature to present effectively; people instinctively become frustrated and disengage when confronted with things that don't make sense. However, slowly turning PCs toward discomfort leaves them with a sense of vulnerability.

SEWING PARTS TOGETHER

Many monsters exhibit more than one nature. A vengeful ghost blends supernatural and human natures, showing calculated cruelty alongside the power of death. A kraken combines the bestial and alien natures to make a creature capable of mass destruction that emerges from unknowable depths. Adam, the monster from Frankenstein, blends three natures, exhibiting themes from human, bestial, and supernatural all at once. Don't feel limited to one realm when making your monsters. Fear is complex, and so are the creatures born from it!

If you want help turning these natures into monstrous traits, roll a d6 four times and choose a few traits from the following table based on the natures you want your monster to have:

Human	Bestial	Supernatural	Alien
1. Plotting	1. Hunting	1. Intangible	1. Complex
2. Vindictive	2. Nesting	2. Inevitable	2. Mindless
3. Cruel	3. Stalking	3. Vast	3. Corrupting
4. Mocking	4. Wild	4. Permanent	4. Unknown
5. Defiling	5. Infesting	5. Periodical	5. Infinite
6. Deceitful	6. Rampaging	6. Ancient	6. Advanced

✎ **Using your results as prompts answer one or more of the following questions:**

- How does this monster select victims?
- What can this monster destroy?
- How could this monster cause injury?
- How could this monster kill?
- Why is this monster difficult to evade?
- What would it take to drive this monster away?
- What goal does this monster have?

Appearance

Monsters are fear given form; they really need to look the part. Nothing drains the power out of a horror movie faster than a monster that doesn't look right. In RPGs we have a little leeway because our monsters live in the players' imaginations. You don't need to completely design a terrifying creature; you just need to give your players enough details so they can make their own nightmares.

✎ **Start by identifying at least three core themes this monster represents. These can be words or phrases:**

Now, take your three core themes and identify six ideas you associate with each of them. Try to sum up your first three associations with specific images like "teeth," "fungus," "hooks," or "fire." For your last three try to use abstract concepts like "decay," "grace," or "magnetism."

1.	2.	3.
1.	1.	1.
2.	2.	2.
3.	3.	3.
4.	4.	4.
5.	5.	5.
6.	6.	6.

Finally, choose two words from any of the lists you previously made. If you can't decide roll two d6 to find them. Once they are selected use those two concepts as inspiration to describe the following aspects of your monster's appearance. Consider how the relationship between prompts connects themes to inform the monster's appearance.

SILHOUETTE

This is a monster's overall frame, how they look when standing in front of a victim. This suggests a monster's strength, reach, and subtlety. A large creature might be powerful, a spindly creature might be difficult to evade, a slight creature might be hard to see or track.

TEXTURE

This defines the look of a monster's skin, exoskeleton, clothing, scales, or fur. It can communicate how tough or unpleasant a creature is. An effective texture makes the audience want to recoil and actually know less.

SENSES

These are the obvious tools your monster has for detecting victims. They can be things like eyes, ears, or antennae. Senses suggest the threat of being discovered but also offer an indication of how the monster interacts with the world. A creature with large eyes is terrifying because it can use them to see you; a creature with a flicking tongue is terrifying because that might be a snakelike weapon.

WEAPONS

This is what your monster uses to inflict harm. It can be an actual part of your monster's body or a tool that they carry. Some weapons are visible all the time; others are concealed until it is time for the monster to strike. Weapons always introduce and heighten danger.

Violence

A monster doesn't just look scary; a creature with a flicking tongue is terrifying because it might be smelling you the way a snake does its prey. Violence justifies all the revulsion and terror we feel when we see a monster, because we understand what it is capable of.

Violence can also exist outside of action. Even if a movie is about a particular monster, the monster usually spends most of its time offscreen. When the monster isn't around, it makes itself known through the results of its acts of violence. PCs often encounter a violent monster first through its deeds, understanding the danger before ever encountering the monster.

THREATENING

This is a type of emotional violence—a way for the monster to erode feelings of safety and security in the PCs through signs and atmospheric phenomena. This kind of violence can herald a monster's impending arrival, show it has passed through, or mark the boundaries of its domain.

✹ **Choose a mode for threatening violence:**

- ○ **Sound:** It can be heard, like the howl of a wolf, the wail of a siren, the roar of a chainsaw, or the thump of footsteps.
- ○ **Sight:** It can be seen, like claw marks, eldritch symbols, shed scales, or ectoplasm.
- ○ **Smell:** It can be smelled, like burnt hair, stagnant water, harsh chemicals, and rotting flesh.
- ○ **Feeling:** It can be felt physically or emotionally, like slimy surfaces, a change in temperature, an overwhelming sadness, or vertigo and nausea.

✹ **When threatening violence appears, choose two:**

- ○ It could easily be attributed to something unrelated.
- ○ It disappears soon after being discovered.
- ○ It implies the PCs are too late in doing something critical.
- ○ It implies the monster is closer than expected.
- ○ It tempts the PCs to take a risk.

MARKING

Marking violence is something lasting that keeps the monster present after it leaves a scene. Any visible injury is technically a type of marking violence. It's more effective if it evokes the monster's specific threat. Examples of violence's mark include the small wounds of a vampire's bite, a tracking collar from an alien creature, or a symbol for a ghost's curse.

✹ **Choose two qualities for marking violence:**

- ○ It makes people distrust the victim.
- ○ It helps the monster track the victim.
- ○ It distorts the victim's perception.
- ○ It makes a simple task extremely difficult.
- ○ It grows or spreads.

TRANSFORMATIVE

This is the most overt and permanent violence a monster can inflict. In many cases this violence is fatal, but it also leads to fates worse than death. It should be dramatic and horrible, underscoring all of a monster's core themes.

☀ **Choose two qualities for transformative violence:**

- ○ It is messy.
- ○ It alters the victim's body temporarily, then permanently.
- ○ It alters the victim's mind temporarily, then permanently.
- ○ It makes the monster more dangerous.
- ○ It furthers a terrible goal.
- ○ It is fatal to the victim.

☀ **Choose a limitation for transformative violence:**

- ○ It takes time to mature.
- ○ It depends on external conditions.
- ○ It has to follow a pattern.
- ○ It requires a specific victim.
- ○ It makes the monster vulnerable.

Vulnerabilities

While you absolutely want players and their characters to view monsters as dangerous, you don't really want your PCs to avoid those dangers completely. Vulnerabilities encourage PCs to engage with a monster on specific terms. The promise of an advantage drives risk—which is great because action and drama love risks.

☀ Choose a type of vulnerability:

○ **Life-giving substances:** Some monsters that represent death are vulnerable to things that provide life and safety like water, sunlight, salt, or certain foods. This sort of vulnerability provides PCs with lots of options to confront the monster and makes awareness of their environment important.

○ **Valuable:** Some monsters are vulnerable to objects that people find valuable like silver, mirrors, and rare herbs. This focuses the PCs on finding specific weapons, adding tension to confrontations.

○ **Approach:** Some monsters are only venerable to certain kinds of violence like beheading, piercing their heart, or disposing of the body in a specific way. This means your PCs will always need a plan.

○ **Story:** A few monsters are vulnerable because of their past, a set of rules, or a specific pattern. This sort of vulnerability requires the PCs to research and understand the monster.

☀ Choose two effects for this vulnerability:

○ Slays or disables the monster instantly.
○ Slays or disables the monster permanently.
○ Repels the monster.
○ Weakens the monster's power.
○ Restricts the monster's movement.

☀ Choose two assets for this vulnerability:

○ It can be carried easily.
○ It can be concealed.
○ It requires no skill or training.
○ It is easy to acquire.
○ It can be reused.
○ It isn't dangerous to people.

☼ **Choose two complications for this vulnerability:**

- ○ It depends on factors the PCs can't control.
- ○ It depends on faith, confidence, or hidden knowledge.
- ○ It takes time to be effective.
- ○ It requires a skill or training to use.
- ○ It becomes depleted with use.
- ○ It is rare or expensive.
- ○ It is dangerous to people.
- ○ It is bulky or cumbersome.

Building a Conspiracy

A good deal of horror focuses on killers and monsters stalking inno-cent victims. However, some stories focus on threats posed by secret groups working toward destructive ends. Cults, secret societies, and other clandestine factions collaborate to abuse their power and pur-sue harmful agendas.

Conspiracies are a great tool for RPGs because they add intrigue, rationalize unexplainable behaviors, and allow the PCs to take dra-matic action without prematurely ending the story. Environments where PCs don't know whom to trust, can't negotiate, and can't solve a problem by killing one bad guy support suspense and drama.

To create an interesting conspiracy for your horror story, assign priorities of 1 to 5 for its **size, influence, ideological danger, supernat-ural connection**, and **dedication** without repeating a number.

Size

This determines how many members a conspiracy has. When choosing the size of your conspiracy it's important to consider how members are gathered. A few thousand conspirators living as one town feels very different than cells of conspirators scattered across the globe.

1. This organization is so massive it feels like there are more people involved than not involved, as though its secret nature is a malicious show orchestrated to make the PCs yearn for a safer world that never existed in the first place.
2. This organization is almost impossible to avoid because they have members everywhere. No matter where PCs go, there are eyes and ears belonging to the conspiracy waiting to find them.
3. This organization is large enough that it has total control of a concentrated area like a town, *or* it has membership in scattered pockets spread out over a large area like a country.
4. This organization ranges between a few dozen and a hundred members. It's an intimidating group but definitely short of an army. They might control a business, religion, or social club.
5. There are less than a dozen members of this conspiracy. Even if others act in its interest, only a handful of people know the full truth.

Influence

This determines how much wealth, institutional power, and respect a conspiracy commands. It indicates what sort of mundane destructive capability a conspiracy has and how they might be held accountable. Almost any conspiracy can organize a crime like a murder, but their influence determines whether or not they can cover up their actions and how hard they need to work in order to do that.

1. This organization controls the power of a large government or megacorporation. They are able to move billions of dollars' worth of resources, and in most situations the laws simply do not apply to them. They are restrained only by the threat that acting conspicuously poses to their plans.

2. This organization can influence heads of state but might not control countries outright. They can move hundreds of millions of dollars in resources, and in many cases they can bend the law to look away from their activities. They are competing with many other powerful organizations and maintain secrecy to protect their assets.
3. This organization can easily gain access to weapons and equipment to make themselves dangerous, but they need time to get anything to conduct major projects. They are still accountable to the law, but only if their crimes are documented.
4. This organization has enough resources to procure weapons and equipment to make themselves dangerous given enough time. They might have influence over one or two people in positions of authority, but they are mostly disconnected from outsiders.
5. This organization has very few resources. They don't have any influence beyond their members and actively have a bad reputation with outsiders.

Ideological Danger

Almost every conspiracy is dangerous because they are based on beliefs people feel they need to hide. This determines how inherently dangerous this conspiracy's core beliefs are to outsiders and members alike.

1. This group aims to reforge the world into a terrible new version of itself. They seek to erode virtues, seize power, and permanently transform society into a machine for misery and horror.
2. This group seeks to bring about the end of the world or worship a similar form of fatalistic violence. Their goals and the steps they are willing to take in order to reach them are dangerous.
3. This group simply seeks to seize and hold power by any means necessary. They are dangerous but only in the mundane way that all selfish and corrupt people are dangerous. They are willing to allow people to come to harm for their own benefit.

4. This group has a zealous belief in a strange ideal. They are not inherently dangerous or intent on committing acts of harm for their own sake, but they are willing to harm in the name of their beliefs.
5. This group isn't exactly dangerous in a traditional sense. The way they see the world is out of step with the rest of society. They might inadvertently serve a more dangerous force or desire things that will make the world worse, but they will not cause harm on their own.

Supernatural Connection

In horror there is always a chance that cults and secret societies actually represent real supernatural threats. This determines how important supernatural forces are to a conspiracy, and how much power they might hold. Even when there is no supernatural threat, occult imagery and language make encountering a conspiracy more unnerving.

1. This conspiracy was formed around a supernatural being of immense cosmic power. Members are shaped and empowered by their connection to this force and may even command monsters that act in its service.
2. This conspiracy has access to magic spells, monstrous creatures, or supernatural powers. Their command of these forces might not be complete, but they have enough to make themselves dangerous.
3. A few members of this organization appear to have extraordinary abilities. They could be supernatural, or they could be the result of drugs, altered mental states, or extreme physical conditioning.
4. If there is a connection to supernatural power, it exists only in occult styling or pseudo-religious rhetoric. They might practice bizarre rituals, use metaphorical language, or identify themselves with strange titles, but there is no actual magic involved.
5. There is nothing even remotely supernatural about this conspiracy. It more closely resembles espionage or a secret society.

Dedication

This determines how faithful conspirators are to their own cause. Some conspiracies involve members willingly harming themselves, committing violent coups, and following leaders without question. Others are just collections of people scheming against the world to seize power. Dedication defines the limits of a conspirator's behavior and what it takes to hold power over them.

1. All of the members of this organization are willing to commit their bodies and souls to their cause. They have absolutely unshakable dedication and are willing to accept fates worse than death to see their mission complete.
2. Nearly everyone in this organization is willing to kill for their cause, and nearly as many are willing to die for it. A portion of devotees might even accept consequences worse than death.
3. The majority of people within this organization are willing to kill or harm outsiders. A portion of them might be willing to die for their beliefs. Almost everyone will believe lies told to them by their superiors without question.
4. There are a few people in this organization who would be willing to kill or harm outsiders, though most would not. The vast majority will not question the word of their superiors and might be deceived into doing things they wouldn't otherwise.
5. The majority of members of this organization are involved for logical and selfish reasons. They only listen to their superiors because they believe this conspiracy will somehow benefit them. Similarly, very few are willing to personally get their hands dirty and will walk away from difficult tasks. There might be a few true believers, but they are the exception and not the rule.

Boom and Bust

It just doesn't feel like a horror world without a really *weird* location. The kind of place that makes you wonder aloud "Who on earth would build something like this!?" This exercise helps you create a fictional history of a strange place, creating details along the way.

A Dream Built on a Nightmare

The story of this place starts with the purchase of a parcel of land by an eccentric person with a dream. This person wants to build something that will bring their dreams to life; however, they don't have unlimited funds and they need a bargain.

 Roll a d8 to see what this place was built on top of:

1. A mine
2. A battlefield
3. A burial ground
4. A plague clinic
5. A cult compound
6. A sanitarium or hospital (closed for misconduct)
7. A prison
8. A slaughterhouse

Despite extensive renovations, there were a few things that couldn't be removed:

🖋 **Use the following prompts to describe details within the space:**

- **Something built around:** This is an artifact of this place's darker history that was too large or unmanageable to be removed. Instead, it was awkwardly incorporated into the new space, a badly concealed reminder of what this place used to be.

- **Something hidden away:** This is a perfectly preserved piece of the past waiting to be unearthed. It was built over, hidden, or sealed away.
- **Something intangible:** This reminder of the past hangs over this place like a shroud that can never be removed. It might be a smell, a noise, or even stories that seem to linger endlessly despite the efforts of new ownership.

 Someone tried to build a dream. Roll a d10 to choose a new business or pick your own:

1. A theme park
2. A theater
3. A circus
4. A church
5. A museum
6. A mall
7. A zoo
8. A hotel
9. A school
10. A home

 A great deal of expense and effort went into building this dream. Roll two d6 to see how successful it was:

1. **On a result of 10 or higher**, this dream was realized almost perfectly before it collapsed.
2. **On a 7–9**, choose one complication from the following list.
3. **On a 6 or less**, choose two complications and add "it was in constant financial peril."

Complications

- ○ A major piece of this place remained unfinished until it closed.
- ○ This place never drew the crowds the owner was hoping to see.
- ○ This place suffered constant vandalism by people who were upset about the past.
- ○ Part of this place required constant maintenance, otherwise it would collapse.
- ○ The owner had to take on a partner who compromised their vision.
- ○ There were incidents that had to be covered up.

Based on the journey so far decide on three iconic aspects of this place in its prime:

- ● **The tower:** A piece of this place's architecture loomed large over the rest of it. It could be seen from almost any location within the world. It's the kind of attraction that gets printed on postcards and promotional posters.

🖋 **What was it?**

- ● **The symbol:** A logo or mascot that appeared on signs, posters, and statues all over the world.

🖋 **What was it?**

- **The promenade:** A massive public space meant to accommodate a very large number of people. The sort of place so designed for human traffic that it is unnerving to see it unpopulated.

✏️ **What was it?**

- **The labyrinth:** A part of this place is infamous for being difficult to navigate and full of places to hide, like a hall of mirrors, hedge maze, or sculpture garden.

✏️ **What was it?**

The Collapse

Of course, to make this a location fit for horror, the dream has to die and decay.

🎲 **Roll a d6 to determine the major reason this place closed:**

1. A natural disaster
2. Local economic collapse
3. Organized crime
4. Self-sabotage by unqualified ownership
5. A deeply emotional and personal tragedy
6. A reason directly related to the horror

What permanent scar did the closing of this place leave on the property?

Decide how many decades this place has remained abandoned. For each decade a different force of decay leaves a mark.

6 **Roll a d6 to find a force and decide how it scars this place:**

1. **Weather:** Forces like wind, rain, flooding, and sunlight changed the way this place looks, making it appear strange and filthy.
2. **Vandalism:** People broke into this property to leave a mark. Some of it is transformative art; some of it is petty destruction.
3. **Nature:** Plants and animals have overgrown different parts of this place, bringing outdoor ecosystems inside.
4. **Squatting:** People for a while tried to make this place a shelter or home. Like the efforts of the previous owners, this eventually failed, but it changed the landscape before it did.
5. **Rot:** Rust, mold, and other forces ate away some part of this place, causing it to warp and break.
6. **Condemnation:** Efforts were made to close off this place from a curious public.

52 Ways to Find a Body

Whether you're dealing with a mundane human killer or a supernatural monster, chances are you're going to end up with a few crime scenes. Forensic investigation is partially about using static evidence to form a narrative. This makes forensic scenes really great tools for horror. It keeps the danger off-screen while letting your PCs' imaginations fill in gaps.

This exercise will help you quickly and easily generate interesting details for crime scenes. Draw from a standard deck of playing cards (jokers included); **color**, **suit**, and **value** of each card will provide you with a prompt to help you build your scene.

Red

Red cards provide your PCs information about the victim of this crime. More often than not, PCs prioritize information about killers and monsters, because they pose direct threats. Encountering death in a horror story represents a glimpse into a possible future. Helping PCs understand and identify with a victim helps them imagine that fate for themselves.

HEARTS

Hearts provide insights into a victim's personality and emotions. Who was this person before they were killed by a monster? What were they doing around a monster in the first place? Were they expecting trouble? All of these questions can be answered by details in hearts.

DIAMONDS

Diamonds provide physical evidence related to the victim's body or possessions. This helps the PCs figure out what happened and how they can better prepare themselves in the future. It also creates an opportunity to give PCs clues to move them toward their next steps.

◉ Follow, Don't Fight

Sometimes interpretation is not always easy and obvious. If you draw the 9 of Hearts, your prompt is "a weapon that relates to the victim's emotions or personality." It might feel more natural to connect a weapon to the killer, and it's much easier to conceive of a weapon as a physical object.

A draw like this can mean the PCs discover evidence that the victim might have been armed, or has an emotional connection to weaponry. Perhaps they were a police officer or a doomsday prepper. Interpretive mechanics are stronger when you challenge yourself to establish unlikely connections.

Black

Black cards provide PCs information about the killer. This is your chance to ramp up tension and give your PCs valuable information that could save their lives. Remember that even bestial monsters have thoughts and plans. It will be easier to create new details if you know there are *reasons* the killer chose to kill—even if they are very simple.

SPADES

Spades provide the PCs information about the killer's motivations and methods. They'll help your group sort out why the killer struck here, how they chose their victim, and where they might go next.

CLUBS

These prompts provide information about the killer's body, abilities, possessions, or location. More than any other suit, clubs will provide PCs a direct line to the monster. As you near the climax of your adventure feel free to provide increasingly concrete information in these draws.

	Prompts
A	There is evidence that confirms a hunch someone in the party has had for a long time.
K	There is an intentional message here. Even if it's not communicating to the party directly, information was left here in hopes someone would find it.
Q	There is something here someone was trying to keep hidden. For some reason they were not able to conceal it.
J	There is information here that establishes a clear relationship between the killer and victim—even if it's a very simple one.
10	There is evidence of a survivor.
9	There is a weapon present.
8	A piece of furniture was damaged.
7	A surface was stained.
6	There is an incomplete message present.
5	There is something that suggests a non-immediate threat to one of the PCs.
4	There is evidence of an injury.
3	There is information that suggests why this character was here.
2	There is evidence that is easy to misinterpret.
JR	There is something that poses an immediate physical danger to one of the PCs.

We suggest drawing one card for each player, including yourself. That will populate the scene with interesting threads without over-complicating it.

Once you have drawn your prompt cards, shuffle them together and place them in front of you facedown. The first card you draw will be the easiest detail to find. Each card after that should be progressively more challenging for PCs to find.

This will provide your party with a nice bell curve of challenge. Don't feel bad if they don't manage to find everything; all that matters is that the PCs have enough to know where to go next.

I Wouldn't Want to Live There

Eventually your PCs need to confront the monster. Forcing them to do that in the monster's lair heightens the drama. Even in the final act of your horror story, environments do a lot of heavy lifting. They can creep out the PCs before they even start the fight.

This exercise walks you through creating a creepy lair for your monster so your PCs have the perfect stage for their showdown.

Make a Foundation
First you'll need to decide on a general location for the monster's lair.

☀ **Choose one descriptor:**

- ○ **Natural:** Somewhere outdoors but still closed in like forests and caves.
- ○ **Residential:** A place built to be a home like a house or apartment.
- ○ **Industrial:** A place built to manufacture or house things, full of machinery.
- ○ **Retail:** A place meant to sell goods of some kind.
- ○ **Public:** A place made for the public to pass through like subways, airports, and parks.

☀ **Choose two descriptors:**

○ Mazelike   ○ Filthy
○ Claustrophobic   ○ Vast
○ Crumbling

How is it cut off from the outside world?

‎

‎

Why is this place unpopulated when the PCs visit?

‎

‎

 Frankenstein That Castle!

You can combine this exercise with Boom and Bust and make a really distinct and eerie stage for your climax!

Do Some Decorating

Now that you have a general idea of what this place is, it's time to add some details! Even without a monster it should be unsettling.

Roll a d20 three times to get prompts for unsettling details:

1. This place feels out of step with time in some way; it's too futuristic or too old-fashioned.
2. There is a sound that occurs frequently here that could easily be mistaken for another person or thing moving through the space.
3. There are objects that cast strange shadows.

4. There is a leak that makes itself known in sight or sound.
5. A critical path is in dangerous disrepair, but only presents a threat if someone moves through without caution.
6. There is graffiti and it looks incomplete.
7. This place feels dirty—there isn't a single surface that you could touch without coming into contact with some sort of grime.
8. This place is home to an odd collection.
9. An animal obviously made a home here.
10. There is a memorial or other reminder of death here.
11. There are lots of places a large person or creature could hide here.
12. There are an unusual number of reflective surfaces here.
13. Wind can easily move objects here.
14. People are forced to contend with narrow passages and corridors when moving through here.
15. Things work, but never on the first try. Door handles need to be jiggled, light switches need to be flicked repeatedly, engines take a while to turn over.
16. A deeply intimate artifact—like a diary or a photo album—is hidden somewhere it can be found.
17. Almost anything PCs do has a noticeable impact on the environment. Walking makes loud footsteps or noticeable prints, touching objects moves dust or breaks fragile things.
18. Mundane items always seem to be arranged in an unusual way—chairs set on a table, books set out and open, cabinets left ajar.
19. The temperature is always a few degrees away from comfortable, either too hot or too cold.
20. There are many objects here that are easy to mistake for human beings when light is bad.

Monster Makeover

To really make it a *lair* the monster has to add a personal touch. The monster's presence needs to be clear as soon as the PCs enter its space. This is more than seeing footprints or claw marks; this is part of the monster's will influencing the environment.

 Roll a d8 to determine how the monster has changed this place:

1. **Preparation:** The monster has made this environment ready to challenge invaders like the PCs.
2. **Infestation:** The monster is reproducing or nurturing more creatures like itself.
3. **Incarceration:** The monster is holding victims here for some sinister purpose.
4. **Re-creation:** The monster has attempted to restore this place to a previous condition or alter it to mimic a faraway place.
5. **Communication:** The monster has embedded a critical story or message into this environment.
6. **Indoctrination:** The monster is preparing to welcome outsiders into its organization or lifestyle by preparing some sort of ceremony or transformation.
7. **Desolation:** The monster has broken or corrupted something here, leaving it in a nightmarish and unrecognizable state.
8. **Transformation:** The monster has somehow altered matter or beings in this space into something strange or unnatural.

People need a reason to go to a place that is so obviously dangerous. The PCs might be there specifically to face danger, but that won't be a lure for most of the monster's other victims. Add something to tempt people.

What valuable thing is held here within the monster's grasp?

The Point of No Return

Finally, the lair needs to offer the PCs one final chance to falter. This is a boundary within the environment that lets the PCs know they have committed to facing the monster instead of trying to escape.

✳ **To determine the nature of the threshold, choose one of the following qualities:**

- ○ **Fragile:** The path will collapse under pressure and seal itself.
- ○ **Uncertain:** The path will change; one cannot go out the way they went in.
- ○ **Treacherous:** There is no way to follow this part of the path in a hurry.
- ○ **Winding:** Unless it is navigated with careful thought, the path always leads back to the inner lair.

One final option is to create a way for this lair to be totally destroyed. This isn't necessary for all horror stories but it is useful for many. If all other plans fail, it gives the PCs the ability to damn the monster alongside themselves, and it creates an ending full of quiet uncertainty.

✎ **What threatens to destroy this place and everyone in it?**

X-Punk

While fantasy, sci-fi, and horror are all literary mainstays, some folks might be wondering what the heck x-punk is. "Punk" fiction explores stories about resisting oppression, often set in dystopian worlds.

While "punk" themes commonly establish these worlds, the character and aesthetic for punk worlds change based on subgenre. Usually subgenres define technology and industry, letting those ideas define the battlefield for resisting oppression. The most recognizable subgenre for punk is "cyberpunk." In this subgenre people struggle for individuality, bodily autonomy, and survival in a world ravaged by corporatism and capitalism empowered by advanced technology.

We use "x" as a variable to stand in for the infinite options you have to create punk worlds. The "x" tells you what the most important tools, skills, and other aesthetics are, so you can more effectively build around them. Check out the subgenres in the Style Is Substance exercise in this chapter if you want to see how they can influence a punk setting.

All of the exercises in this chapter are designed to help you build essential punk themes into your world, while still giving you the freedom to build whatever you want.

d20 Questions

The most important aspect of punk is the dynamic among three groups: **oppressors**—the ruling classes that dictate the laws of society; **the oppressed**—everyone under the power of the ruling classes;

and **punks**—people who reject society and get forced to the fringes, occasionally actively resisting oppressors. Without this dynamic, your world will be missing the soul of punk.

These questions will help establish that dynamic before you start building it out with the exercises.

 Roll a d20 for each player (including yourself) and answer the corresponding question:

1. What style of music influences the attitude of this world?
2. What style of art or architecture influences the look of this world?
3. What do people consider the most dangerous place in this world?
4. What dangerous luxury exists in this world?
5. What vital resource is rare in this world?
6. How long ago did the oppressors rise to power?
7. Whom do people talk about when they are sure no one is listening?
8. What represents freedom to the oppressed?
9. Whom do the oppressors fear most?
10. What event do oppressors wish they could make everyone forget?
11. Where do oppressors house dissidents?
12. Does anyone live outside the system of oppression? If so, who?
13. How do punks keep themselves safe?
14. What talents or skills are considered especially valuable in this world?
15. What mundane luxury is scarce and controlled?
16. Do people modify their bodies? If so, how?
17. What is the most common form of transportation? Is that answer different for oppressors?
18. What part of this world feels penned in and small? What part of this world feels vast and mysterious?
19. How do oppressors threaten, seduce, and control people?
20. What represents hope to the oppressed? How do punks celebrate this?

Style Is Substance

There are two essential elements in every punk story:

1. Resisting oppression
2. Style

The relative importance of these elements doesn't necessarily have to be in that order.

You may have wondered, when watching a movie, things like: "Why are characters wearing armor that doesn't protect vital areas?" "Why do characters wear goggles they don't ever use?" "Why is a clandestine resistance leader—who wants to avoid detection—covered in bright neon lights?" These are all examples of punk settings putting style over practicality.

It seems silly, but it all makes a point about the world and the characters in it. Punk isn't about wearing garbage bags and combat boots because it's easy or comfortable. It's about making a statement.

Subgenre

Starting from scratch, punk can look like a tangled mess. Themes and aesthetics are so closely tied that it can be difficult to tell which is leading and which is following. Those roles might even shift back and forth throughout your worldbuilding process.

We called this chapter of *The Ultimate RPG Game Master's Worldbuilding Guide* "X-Punk" because there are an infinite number of subgenres that fit the punk structure and can be used as a prefix with "punk." Sometimes subgenres define aesthetic elements of the world. This means it's possible for two punk worlds to look and feel very different and still be in the same genre.

For example, most cyberpunk stories are set in near-future dystopias. In these worlds, rampant corporatism and capitalism have warped society into something that no longer values people as individuals. These stories explore anxieties around emergent technology and its effect on society. Most foundational fiction for this subgenre came from the late 1960s to the 1980s, so the aesthetics are based on counterculture movements of those eras.

Dieselpunk combines midcentury modern aesthetics with a yearning for frontiers and a sense of self-sufficient individualism. Heroes in these settings are nomadic wanderers who never settle and embrace a difficult life on the road. Everyone who settles to live in a single place becomes either corrupt or prey for the corrupt. Dieselpunk pulls inspiration from Westerns and industrial labor conflicts of the 1920–1950s era.

Cyberpunk and dieselpunk are both examples of punk fiction, and they both pit defiant iconoclasts clashing with a cruel ruling class. However, cyberpunk's claustrophobic supercities look nothing like dieselpunk's barren wastelands.

If you already have a subgenre in mind, be aware that it carries thematic and aesthetic elements that can have a dramatic impact on the way your world looks and feels. That's a good thing! You can use those existing themes as a foundation. The following table lists different punk subgenres and their thematic elements. This will help you see the different approaches to punk fiction.

Subgenre	Aesthetic Elements	Thematic Elements
Cyberpunk	• Technology • Body modification • Retro subcultures: punks, goths, etc. • Neon • Retro computing • Urban environments • Synth music • Broken environment	• Toxic capitalism • Corporate authority over legal authority • Information warfare • Disposable humanity • Monopolization • Loss of individuality • Oppression of conformity

Subgenre	Aesthetic Elements	Thematic Elements
Steampunk	• 1700s–1800s fashion • Pre- to early-industrial technology • Steam and coal power • Retro futurism • Lenses, gears, springs, and coils • Brass and copper fixtures • Decorative utility • Historical figures	• Colonialism, imperialism, royalism • Oppressed factory classes • Exploration and discovery • Competitive invention • Looming threat of warring powers • Alternate history
Dieselpunk	• Fashion from 1940s–1960s • Cars, motorcycles, engine-based technology • Large wild environments • Grease, smoke, and tools • Pomade, makeup, radio	• Unions vs. corporate authority • Lawlessness in wastelands • Pollution causing environmental disaster • Rigid social and economic castes • Youth vs. age
Necropunk	• Bones, organs, blood • Outdated medical equipment • Early anatomical drawings • Magic • Skeletons, zombies, and other undead things • Memento mori macabre • Funerary clothing • Latin and medical terminology	• Death vs. immortality • The price of knowledge and power • The power of study and practice • Royalism • Disposability of human life • The fragility of life • Famine, pestilence, wasting • Rigid social castes • Regency politics

Subgenre	Aesthetic Elements	Thematic Elements
Apocalyptic Punk	• Ruins of civilization • Inhospitable landscapes • Scrap and trash refashioned into clothing and tools • Imagery-of-violence weapons as decoration • Filth, grime, and dust • Scarring, mutation, disfiguration	• Breakdown of society • Scarcity and scavenging • Loss of knowledge and culture • Worship of violence • Fear of other people • Consequences of environmental destruction
Dungeon-punk	• Faux medieval fashion • Swords, bows, axes, and magic • Nonhuman sentient creatures • Castles, forts, dungeons, caves • Monsters	• Royalism • Intercultural conflict • Discovery, wonder, exploration • Scavenging fragments of a lost civilization • Mythology

It's also okay to mix and match; start with your favorite themes and aesthetics and create your own unique subgenre.

Once you have a subgenre, consider pairing it with a musical, artistic, cultural, or historical movement to help inform your punk's sense of style. All those expressive movements have themes of their own that will help shape the style and substance of your world.

◉ Example: Punk World

World name: Bone Music

Subgenre: Necropunk/Jazzpunk

Inspiration:
- Medical and death imagery
- Jazz and swing
- Bootleg records made from x-ray prints that were used to smuggle Western music into the Soviet Union after World War II

Oppressive sorcerers control the world and have developed the Rabofon, a device that uses sounds to puppeteer people by their bones and force them into labor. The Dancers are an underground group that appropriate the magic to free themselves and fight their oppressors.

Clash with the World

Punk protagonists need to stick out. Even in a world that looks very different than our own, it should be easy to understand whom the story is about by seeing the difference between punks and their oppressors. Many cyberpunk stories pit business-suit executives and cops in riot gear against outlaws in leather and neon who would look at home in a nightclub. Steampunk settings feature opulently dressed land- and factory-owning nobility against a machine-operating labor class.

The style choices made by punks are a response to the world around them. This can mean punks subverting societal expectations or embracing and owning expectations.

The oppressors in cyberpunk want to turn the world into an office and refuse to look at the working class. In response cyberpunks dress in a loud, unprofessional way. On the other hand, punks in steampunk might stitch gears into their clothes to protest the way nobility sends the working class to be mangled by machines in factories, sending the message that "now these teeth are coming for you."

Look

Punk protagonists literally wear their feelings and beliefs. To make a punk world you need to figure out what the protagonists are trying to say because that tells you how they will look.

CALL ME UGLY

This piece of your punk aesthetic is focused around taking control of the things oppressors force on the oppressed. If society celebrates extravagance, this part of the look focuses on simplicity. If society looks down on laborers, it celebrates a signifier of the working class. If society demands neatness, this element is messy and chaotic.

This works best as:
- A small accessory like jewelry, piercings, and makeup
- A hairstyle
- A tattoo

☀ **Select a statement this element makes:**

- ◯ When you made me wear this it was yours; now it's mine.
- ◯ I only play your games when you're watching.
- ◯ I'll always show you what you hate.
- ◯ You tried to cast me out, and set me free.

☀ **Select two aesthetic elements:**

- ◯ It is sharp with jagged edges.
- ◯ It is bright and loud.
- ◯ It is delicate and precious.
- ◯ It is tacky and unrefined.
- ◯ It is aggressive and fatalistic.
- ◯ It is romantic and poetic.
- ◯ It is joyous and hopeful.
- ◯ It is colorful and flowing.

○ It is muted and geometric.
○ It is utilitarian and unpretentious.
○ It is simple and natural.

What material or method used to make this element exists only in this world?

When does this element get a punk into trouble? When does it earn them a welcome?

Describe this element:

WHAT I DO

This celebrates something the punks love. Usually this is something that oppressors consider taboo or dangerous. This part of the look serves a utility without being an actual tool.

This works best as:
- A minor accessory like shoes, belts, glasses, and gloves
- A general cut of clothing like skintight fit, baggy layers, or crisp lines
- A modification to the body

☀ Choose two statements this element makes:

- ○ I see beauty few seek out.
- ○ I know what I want the future to look like.
- ○ I have a skill that makes me dangerous.
- ○ I know things most people don't.
- ○ I fight battles most people refuse to see.
- ○ I dream of something people think is impossible.

☀ Select two truths that accompany those statements:

- ○ I'm involved with something illegal.
- ○ I was the victim of a historic tragedy.
- ○ I have never known safety.
- ○ I need to hide what I love most.
- ○ I'm not afraid of a fight.

✎ What does this element help a punk do?

✎ What assumptions do nonpunks make when they see people styled this way?

✎ Describe this element:

WHO I AM

This piece is an iconic signifier of a community and identity. Even if you separate this object from the person it belongs to, you should be able to get a picture of who that person is.

This works best as:
- A large and visible clothing item like a jacket, cloak, or cape
- Armor
- A mask or helmet

☀ **Choose a statement this element makes:**

- ○ I am a threat to the establishment.
- ○ I am part of a movement.
- ○ I can see a future I control.

☀ **Select two advantages that accompany that statement:**

- ○ Like-minded allies
- ○ Supernatural abilities
- ○ A valuable and dangerous skill
- ○ Idealistic clarity
- ○ Freedom from an oppressive tool

✎ **Is this something a person can wear openly? If not, does its concealment protect its wearer's identity?**

✎ **Does it grant power or imply power?**

📝 **Describe the element:**

Tools

Punk often follows working classes exercising their power against oppressors. This makes tools an essential icon of the genre. If the tools your characters use say something about the world, PCs will reinforce your story themes with every action they take.

COMMUNICATION

Every revolutionary movement needs to communicate to proliferate. How a person communicates also helps them define their identity. Since punk is all about crafting a movement around an identity, compelling tools of communication are extremely useful to anchor your world.

✳ **Choose two advantages:**

- ⭘ The material needed for this tool is common, and its use does not arouse suspicion.
- ⭘ Oppressors are mostly unfamiliar with how this tool works.
- ⭘ This tool allows characters to communicate with a large number of people simultaneously.
- ⭘ Using this tool protects a character's anonymity in most cases.
- ⭘ This tool is especially good for passing on critical information or skills.

☀ Choose two drawbacks:

- ○ Use of this tool requires characters to expend a resource.
- ○ Use of this tool leaves a distinct physical mark on the user.
- ○ Communication through this tool is extremely limited in a specific way.
- ○ There are special requirements that need to be met in order to effectively use this tool.
- ○ During or after use of this tool, the user is left temporarily exposed or otherwise vulnerable.

☀ Choose one quirk:

- ○ This tool enables communication through an unusual sense.
- ○ This tool manifests differently for each user.
- ○ Use of this tool is accompanied by some kind of flashy noticeable phenomena.
- ○ There is an uncontrollable outside force that has influence over this tool.

Based on your choices, describe this tool:

DEFENSE

Not every punk story needs to involve physical violence. For those that do, it's important to recognize the difference between violence done by oppressors and violence done by punks. When punks take violent actions, they are appropriating the tools of their oppressors and protecting the things that are important to them. When building weapons for your protagonists be aware of the struggle these tools represent and let them reflect the struggle in form and function.

☀ **Choose two advantages:**

- ○ This tool is appropriated from the system of oppression and turns that power against oppressors.
- ○ This tool can be easily hidden.
- ○ This tool is connected to and powered by the will of the resistance.
- ○ This tool is something oppressors refuse to use.
- ○ This tool can also be used to reverse or correct the harm done by oppressors.

☀ **Choose two drawbacks:**

- ○ This tool can only be used to fight for a limited period of time.
- ○ Anyone who uses this tool to fight has to endure discomfort or hardship.
- ○ This tool is only effective if the user is in a state of emotional or idealistic clarity.
- ○ This tool is powered by a valuable resource.
- ○ This tool relies upon mastery of a specialized skill.

✹ Select three words to describe how this tool looks:

- O Colorful
- O Shining
- O Flashy
- O Elegant
- O Compact
- O Hulking
- O Dangerous
- O Wicked
- O Rusted
- O Worn
- O Humble
- O Intricate
- O Hefty
- O Occult
- O Ramshackle
- O Ancient
- O Modern
- O Ethereal
- O Alien

✹ Select three words to describe how this tool moves or acts:

- O Graceful
- O Precise
- O Volatile
- O Subtle
- O Forceful
- O Brutal
- O Devastating
- O Gentle
- O Plodding
- O Ferocious
- O Spiritual
- O Magical
- O Passionate
- O Utilitarian
- O Otherworldly

Based on your choices, describe this tool:

SELF-MODIFICATION

Punk narratives are closely tied to themes of identity and expression. Many settings support these themes by giving characters the ability to change their physical bodies to better reflect their personalities and pursue their goals.

☀ **Choose two advantages:**

- These tools can enhance a person's physical abilities.
- These tools make changing one's physical appearance a casual choice.
- These tools can help a person recover from illness and injury.
- These tools make people capable of totally new experiences.
- These tools enhance a skill or interest.

☀ **Choose two difficulties:**

- These tools require invasive procedures to adopt.
- These tools require a resource to function properly.
- Use of these tools is obvious to outside observers.
- This tool can only be used in specific circumstances.
- These tools take time to work.

☀ **Choose one:**

- **Native anatomical:** Mimics an existing body part.
- **Non-native anatomical:** Looks like a body part from a different type of living creature.
- **Non-anatomical:** Doesn't look like a body part at all.
- **Abstract:** Something expressed as light, color, or other non-physical stuff.

✸ **Choose one:**

- ○ **Physical:** Actually modifies a physical form.
- ○ **Metaphysical:** Modifies an intellectual, spiritual, or magical form.
- ○ **Projected:** Doesn't actually change form but changes perception of form, like a hologram.

✸ **Choose one:**

- ○ **Subtle:** Hidden or seamlessly integrated into a body.
- ○ **Obvious:** Easy to see this is artificial or added to the body.

✸ **Select one or more keywords to craft a look:**

- ○ **Flora:** Elements from plants like leaves, bark, and petals.
- ○ **Fauna:** Using elements from animals like claws, feathers, and fur.
- ○ **Elemental:** Using raw elemental materials like water, stone, and fire.
- ○ **Altered biological:** Using raw biological components like flesh, bone, and sinew outside their normal biological context.
- ○ **Machine:** Using mechanical components like pulleys, clockwork, and robotics.
- ○ **Arcane:** Using magical components like magical energy, animated objects, and runes.
- ○ **Occult:** Using strange supernatural components like ghosts, demons, and eerie symbols.
- ○ **Particulate:** Using many small components to form a larger whole.

✎ **Describe a popular modification:**

Attitude

The last critical element of punk fiction is the personality that punks project. In many ways the punk persona is an idealized version of yourself standing out against an imperfect world. Attitude defines personal and community behavior.

OUTSIDERS

Society rejects and even fears punks because they challenge established values. Some punks lean in to the shock they inspire in outsiders, using their reputation to shield themselves. Punks can also reject these fears by challenging society with radical approachability.

 What do oppressors tell people about punks?

Decide which of these messages your punks *own* and which they *reject*. Now it's time to figure out how punks communicate their ownership or rejection of these ideas through behavior.

Roll three d6 or choose from this list of behaviors:

1. **Language:** Slang, dialect, and other ways of speaking that emphasize a group's approachability.
2. **Greeting:** The way punks choose to initiate interaction with outsiders. Do they ignore or refuse to acknowledge people? Do they aggressively rebuke and harass people? Do they shout welcome invitations to passersby?
3. **Pastime:** What people do in public sends a strong message to people around them. Music circles might signify a group is welcoming and friendly. Acts of vandalism and destruction project aggressive strength.

4. **Iconography:** We've already talked about how punks dress, but themes can also be expressed through decoration. What kind of symbols show up in punk tattoos, stickers, patches, and graffiti? Skulls and fists send a different message than rainbows and flowers.
5. **Taboo:** Punks develop a sense of propriety within their own community that differs from the outside world. What do punks see as anathema? What do punks practice that outsiders reject?
6. **Music:** Many punks root their identity and beliefs in music. What emotions do the sound and lyrics of a punk's music focus on? How does this sound affront or entice outsiders?

Pair your chosen behaviors with the following statements.

Then decide how this behavior leans in to or rejects the messages of oppressors:

I use _____ to ward against oppressors.

I use _____ to identify friends.

I use _____ to understand myself.

INITIATION

Punks offend oppressors with their very existence, and that can get them killed or worse. They can't afford to trust everyone who tries to join their group. They never know who might be an oppressor trying to infiltrate. They survive by creating rituals to test newcomers.

Determine what sort of community your punks have:

- **Marginalized:** These punks don't really want to be punks. They are forced into a community because there is nowhere else they can go. Their identity is based more on grim acceptance of their differences than on resistance to authority. They might openly live as second-class citizens or try to hide themselves. Either way they are always at risk of being targeted by enforcers. Their rituals are about exposing and confronting the traits that make them outsiders everywhere else.

- **Underground:** These punks opt in to an illicit lifestyle. They resist society's rules as a symbolic gesture rather than a happenstance or ethos. They care more about interacting with people who see the world the way they do than accomplishing any particular goal. Underground punks tend to face legal consequences if they are discovered, so they conceal their identities to move through mainstream society. Others immerse in the punk persona as a declaration of power. Their rituals are about pushing boundaries and displaying authenticity.

- **Radical:** These punks dedicate themselves to open rebellion against their oppressors. Their community is a mix of people who chose this path and folks who were forced into it. They act to destroy or impede oppressors with the hopes of changing society. They are usually killed if discovered and need to conceal their identities or hide their community completely. Their rituals are about proving dedication and furthering a goal.

If you are having trouble deciding what sort of punk community you want, you can roll for it!

First answer these questions:

☀ **Is this community defined by an ideology?**
   ○ Yes   ○ No

☀ **Is this community actively clashing with oppressors?**
   ○ Yes   ○ No

☀ **Is this community willing to use violence?**
   ○ Yes   ○ No

☀ **Does this community have a goal?**
   ○ Yes   ○ No

6 Roll two d6 and add 1 for every time you answered with "yes." Determine your community based on your results:

1. **On a 6 or lower:** Mostly marginalized; choose two from the "Marginalized" column of the table.
2. **On a 7–9:** Mostly underground; choose two from "Underground" or one "Underground" and one "Marginalized."
3. **On a 10 or higher:** Mostly radical; choose two "Radical," one "Radical" and one "Underground," or one of each.

Marginalized	Underground	Radical
• Understand a difficult truth • Face a terrible fear • Take risks when it matters most • Give up a false comfort • Share a painful secret	• Spread an unpopular truth • Take a big risk for little reward • Adopt a mark society hates • Steal something from oppressors • Abandon a comfortable life	• Attack a popular lie • Hurt or kill an oppressor • Face a terrible punishment • Take risks for an idea • Destroy a comforting distraction

Is this something done alone, with a group, or with a partner?

Is this the same every time, or does it change?

How could someone fail?

Enforcers

Police and security personnel are the face of oppression in punk. For our purposes we'll call these groups enforcers, both to keep the setting neutral and to distinguish fictional institutions from the real-world entities. Enforcers impose the will of the powerful on the powerless. They are emblematic of the central struggle of your story and one of the most dynamic aspects of that theme. That means you want them to look and feel right!

◎ Authority Issues

When writing punk it's important to remember it's about abusive authority. Your story might have good folks in tough situations, but anyone comfortable is making compromises. Police and anyone else "keeping the peace" are doing it on behalf of a cruel machine. Punk examines nuance on an individual level and becomes reductive when looking at a group. This means—in this genre—all cops are bastards.

Lies Are Truth

When creating a new aspect of setting it's important to ensure your core themes are the foundation for your new creation. If you're playing with cyberpunk, your enforcers are probably wage slaves of a megacorporation, defending the company's interests at the expense of people. If your setting is swordpunk, enforcers might be a motley crew of brigands who follow a bloody warlord. A flintpunk setting might call for squads of red coat colonial masters who invade populated lands and tax the people they force to live in their settlements.

✎ **Ask yourself the following questions:**

- Who is in power?
- Whom do they steal from?

The answer to those questions shapes the larger thematic framework for your story.

The next thing you'll need to know is what lie the oppressors want people out of power to believe. This will become part of the central mission statement for your enforcers. Picture it as a phrase printed on a propaganda poster.

Here are some examples:
- The Emperor Is God
- Only We Keep You Safe
- We Manufacture the Future
- Civilization Is Refinement
- Strength Is Virtue
- Silence Is Respect
- Obedience Makes Us All Powerful
- Prosperity Belongs to the Just
- Fuel the Fire That Lights the World

The goal of these lies is to pacify resistance and justify brutality. If people believe them, they will fail to act in their own self-interest and may even *support* their oppressors. These lies also form the foundation of how oppressive forces present themselves.

It's okay to create more than one lie your oppressors want the oppressed to believe. Try to narrow your vision to no more than three. Communicating simple messages through design is easier and more effective.

🖉 **Lies:**

Dressed to Kill

Enforcers aren't a vessel for subtlety; they are a canvas upon which oppressing forces loudly declare what they want the world to see. With that in mind, think of how to visually communicate your oppressor's lies.

A cyberpunk megacorps that wants to project "We Manufacture the Future" will make an overt effort to give their enforcers futuristic uniforms. Picture a squad of rent-a-cops in matching suits with clean lines, no visible fasteners, and LEDs highlighting their gear. Like most corporations, they will brand their property with a logo and might even have trademark symbols on their gear.

A steampunk noble might be trying to project "The Emperor Is God" and "Prosperity Belongs to the Just." The uniforms of their enforcers will have signifiers of wealth and divinity incorporated into the design. Perhaps they have bold colors, gold piping and lace, all surrounding religious symbols. Decorating enforcers with sacred imagery and the trappings of wealth reinforces the connection between the ruling classes, prosperity, and religious authority.

With this in mind, it's time to make some choices!

STYLE

※ **Choose one or two forms for your enforcers to fit your themes:**

○ **Military:** Uniforms are slightly more decorated versions of military outfits, practical with lots of epaulets, badges, patches, and piping. A large group will look like toy soldiers.

○ **Futurist:** Uniforms represent an idealized world (from an oppressor perspective). They will look almost alien compared to the civilians around them, lessening the humanity of the officers inside. A large group looks like a line of action figures or tech products.

○ **Ecclesiastic:** These uniforms are based on church authority, with religious symbols and decorations. Depending on the religion they could include flowing, draping fabrics cinched and cut to allow free movement. A large group might look like a choir.

- **Proletarian:** These uniforms are made to imitate the dress of working classes. They have drab colors and a mass-produced feel. A large group looks like workers lined up on a factory floor.
- **Thematic:** It's less of a traditional uniform and more like house or team colors. A distinct manner of dress and self-decoration that makes members unmistakable. Tattoos, skulls, capes, masks, and other emblematic symbols on top of varied bodies and clothes. A large group looks like a mob or gang.
- **Subtle:** Sometimes an oppressor just wants people to think they might be everywhere. Their uniforms are limited to a single symbol of authority like a badge or crest that can be hidden and revealed. A large group looks like an ordinary crowd.

PERSONHOOD

One of the biggest choices you need to make is how "human" enforcers are allowed to look. There is a big difference between a beat cop and a riot cop. Depending on the goals of an enforcer organization they will have varying levels of anonymity and personhood in uniform design.

☀ **Choose an identity for your enforcers:**

- **Open:** Despite the uniforms, it's obvious these are ordinary people representing a larger power. You'll see faces, limbs, and skin. All they need to be enforcers are the right clothes.
- **Obscured:** The humanity of enforcers is warped or slightly altered using masks, tattoos, makeup, or body modification. You can easily tell they are people, but their personhood is underneath decoration.
- **Concealed:** All human elements are hidden behind clothing and decoration. Officers wear helmets, gloves, masks, and armor to completely cover any evidence of humanity.
- **Absent:** The humanity of enforcers is entirely absent. Perhaps enforcers are robots, golems, zombies, or cyborgs that are completely controlled, mind and body, by the oppressors.

Once you have made your choices, it's time to put them together. Blending different ideas may seem difficult, but even seemingly disparate themes can make a cohesive thematic form. Describe the uniforms for your enforcers:

Violence

In a punk setting the way your enforcers enact violence is part of their design. Your narration of attacks against PCs, punks, and civilians will focus on enforcers and their equipment often, so you'll want versatile and dynamic images.

⊙ **Thematic Language**

> **Having iconic tools of violence will also help you signal to your players what the stakes are. If nonlethal weapons are batons and lethal weapons are guns, narrating a description for one or the other as enforcers enter the scene will tell your PCs what kind of conflict they're about to have.**

NONLETHAL

Even in a dystopia where people are routinely executed, it's still good to have nonlethal options, such as saps, clubs, gases, rubber bullets, tasers, armored gloves, black bags, restraints, sedatives, hypnosis, whips, chains, and gun butts. It gives you control over the stakes of your story and allows your enforcers to commit less extreme acts of cruelty.

☀ **Choose two qualities for nonlethal violence:**

- ◯ It always leaves a mark on its victims.
- ◯ It targets multiple victims at once.
- ◯ It's obviously very painful.
- ◯ It makes a sound or smell when readied.
- ◯ It's small and easy to conceal.

Once you have selected a form for nonlethal violence, describe it and where enforcers carry it:

LETHAL

Every enforcer needs the capacity to kill. Stories are driven by characters; oppressors are more effective if they can take people away alongside wealth and power. The way your setting expresses lethal violence says a lot about your oppressors.

Some settings benefit from dispassionate violence like pulling a trigger on a gun. It makes killing easy and automatic, creating distance between the enforcer and the results of their actions. Other settings do better with enforcers who inflict personal cruelty like cutting down a victim with a sword or bayonet.

Your enforcers don't need to always kill with their iconic lethal weapon. It is simply the physical manifestation of their capacity to kill. It should be present in scenes where they are likely to take lives.

☀ **Choose two qualities for your lethal violence:**

- ○ It always leaves evidence behind.
- ○ It is worn prominently by enforcers.
- ○ It is fetishized in imagery on enforcer property.
- ○ It is loud, bright, or both.
- ○ It disfigures victims in a notable way.

Once you have selected a form for nonlethal violence, describe it and where enforcers carry it:

◉ Everything Flows to the Top

Try to make symbols of violence issued by the oppressing body. Anyone can kick someone, so having enforcers kick victims divorces their violence from the larger system. A stunclub manufactured by a megacorps, a phaser issued by a galactic empire, or a spell powered by a totem are thematically stronger because the capacity for violence is provided by the oppressor. If you want kicking and punching to stay in the mix, give your enforcers steel-toed boots, brass knuckles, or metallic limbs.

EMOTIONAL

Emotional violence is often overlooked. Most people see violence as physical. However, emotional violence is extremely useful in storytelling. It's a way to keep oppression in the mind of the audience even when there are no oppressors present. Tools of emotional violence remind the masses that the oppressing power is watching. They can herald the arrival of enforcers or boldly proclaim their presence. Examples of tools of emotional violence include flashing lights, chants, songs, announcements over loudspeakers, holograms, alarms, sirens, bells, trumpets, whistles, and the sound of marching.

Tools of emotional violence thrive in simplicity, and you might find yourself needing more than one. Try to create one based on sight and one based on sound.

✎ **Sight:**

✎ **Sound:**

Moves

Now that you have the basic design for enforcers, it's time to link their look and themes to actions that will create tension in your story. Enforcers are a moving part of the scenery in punk settings. Their mere existence is an active threat against PCs; the way they exist should offend the core of your protagonists.

EXERCISE AUTHORITY

Ownership and control are the goals for oppressors even in situations where those ideas are ill-defined. How can a tyrannical baron own a bridge if the only people who use it are peasants? Does a dogmatic church official really command parishioners if they feel welcome to think and believe things outside church teachings? Enforcers are tasked with performative displays of authority that serve no purpose other than to create authority where there is none.

 Roll a d6 to determine a display of authority for your enforcers:

1. **Observation:** Observation exercises authority by declaring enforcers have knowledge of the events within a specific space, either directly with guards or indirectly with cameras, microphones, and other surveillance equipment.
2. **Bureaucracy:** Bureaucracy exercises authority by requiring the enforcers to legitimize simple activities. Transit, gathering, or business might require paperwork, licenses, or identification.
3. **Interrogation:** Interrogation exercises authority by giving enforcers the right to information. Enforcers expect people to answer questions and volunteer information. Questions can be invasive or noninvasive. Asking for basic information is still interrogation.

4. **Restriction:** Restriction exercises authority by limiting access to resources. This is one of the most direct uses of authority; it declares ownership by making something explicitly exclusive. Guards, barricades, and police tape limit mobility and access for oppressors.

5. **Confiscation:** Through confiscation enforcers limit the ability of the oppressed to "own" in the way oppressors do. Confiscation makes it clear that anything owned by individuals is allowed at the pleasure of the oppressing body.

6. **Violence:** Violence exercises authority by compromising the safety of individuals. Any resistance to violence is met with more forceful violence from enforcers. This is the most direct form of authority, proclaiming that only the oppressors are entitled to feelings of security and safety.

Various displays of authority can overlap. An interrogation might call for bureaucracy in the form of requesting an ID; confiscation might be carried out through violence. As long as you have a clear idea of what your enforcers are doing within a scene, it's okay to blur some lines.

Once you know how authority is being displayed, decide how that display affects the PCs:

- **Targeted:** This display directly vexes the PCs in their efforts. They will have to change plans or be willing to suffer greater consequences for acting against authority.
- **General:** This display will only affect PCs if they make specific decisions. It might cause PCs inconvenience.
- **Background:** This display will not affect PCs unless they go out of their way to intervene.

6 Finally, roll a d6 to see what sort of violence enforcers use to support this display:

1. **1–3: Emotional:** This is more performative than anything else. They hope to intimidate people but don't intend to get physical unless provoked.
2. **4–5: Nonlethal:** There is an urgency or tension driving this action. Enforcers have a specific purpose for this display, and they will harm individuals to carry it out. There is a possibility to navigate this situation without violence, but enforcers are prepared to escalate.
3. **6: Lethal:** The situation is waiting to explode. Lethal violence is present from the start. If there is the appearance of authority being challenged, lives will be lost.

◉ Plot Hole

Some struggle to portray emotional violence. How can you display violence when a scene specifically isn't supposed to lead to physical altercation?

Emotional violence can scale up just like physical violence. A riot cop shouting and *holding* a gun is different from a riot cop shouting while *pointing* a gun *at* someone. You can elevate emotional violence by making threats more intense or personal.

ALLOW CORRUPTION

In a punk setting, laws exist to serve the interests of the oppressors. Oppressors insist that they create a safe and orderly society, but it's an excuse to justify a system that allows them to seize resources and control resistance. Laws are always flexible depending on the needs of oppressors. Enforcers can't be trusted to observe laws to the letter.

This move will help you and your fellow players find the weaknesses in the system. Some of these weaknesses will benefit the PCs, pitting the hollow cynicism of the system against the oppressors.

Others will demonstrate the innate inequity of a broken system, rein-forcing the punk setting.

 When confronted with an institution or system you'd like to corrupt, roll two d6:

1. **On a 6 or lower**, PCs choose two questions for the GM to answer.
2. **On a 7–9**, the GM and PCs choose one question for the other to answer.
3. **On a 10 or higher**, the GM chooses two questions for the PCs to answer.

In all cases it is the GM's goal to answer in a way that demon-strates how the oppressors live above the law, and the PC's goal to demonstrate how inauthentic enforcement allows resistance to sub-vert authority.

Questions

- What do enforcers value more than duty?
- Which conflicts does this system provoke?
- What happens away from watchful eyes?
- What would make this less complicated for enforcers?
- What exceptions are enforcers compelled to observe?

PRACTICE CRUELTY

Enforcers are cruelty personified. They serve a cruel system, designed to benefit cruel people, through cruel behavior. That is meant to call punks to action.

Sometimes it is difficult to compel PCs to act. Their concern for their characters and resources outweighs their need to strike against oppression. While this is an understandable instinct, it is the antithe-sis of punk. This move will help keep punk PCs true to spirit.

Enforcers are capable of two kinds of cruelty: **compelled** and **enabled**. Compelled cruelty is something required of enforcers by the oppressing system. It's the natural result of a bad system behaving as intended.

Enabled cruelty is the result of individuals choosing to exploit a broken system. It's not inherent to the design of the system, but the system allows it.

6 **To spur action in PCs by galling them with cruelty perpetrated by enforcers, roll two d6:**

1. **On a result of 6 or lower**, choose one prompt from the following list; it is carried out against someone within the PC's sight.
2. **On a 7–9**, choose up to two prompts to create a cruelty meant to directly offend one of the PCs' sense of justice.
3. **On a 10 or higher**, choose up to two prompts and use them to have enforcers inflict a cruelty directly against a PC. On an odd result the cruelty is compelled; on an even result the action is enabled.

☀ **Cruelty prompts:**

- ○ Insult someone.
- ○ Break something precious.
- ○ Steal something valuable.
- ○ Strike someone vulnerable.
- ○ Demand something difficult.

Slangs and Arrows

Slang is an extremely versatile worldbuilding tool. The way we speak is a reflection of the world we live in. It would be as out of place for a character in a Shakespearean tragedy to describe their enemy as a "hipster doofus" as it would be for one of your friends to say their ex's new boyfriend is "an odious knave."

In role-playing, speech is our deepest connection to our characters and world. It is often the only thing that happens in the game that also happens in the real world. Speaking like your characters deepens your connection to them.

In the real world, subcultures use slang to communicate within their community and define their identity. That's why developing slang is perfect for x-punk!

This exercise will generate prompts to help you appropriate words to use for slang terms.

Something Good

The word "cool" has been around as an unambiguous term of approval, aspiration, or acclaim since at least the 1920s. There are synonyms for this use of "cool" that have come in and out of favor over time: wizard, groovy, funky, radical, extreme, boss, sweet, fierce, and more.

Making a word as timeless and iconic as "cool" is almost impossible. However, making a word that feels current and tied to a particular group is much easier.

Draw a card from a standard deck of playing cards (jokers included) to find a prompt for a word or phrase that can replace "cool" in specific instances based on the suit and value of your card.

SUITS

- **Spade:** Describing a state of mind or way of being that makes someone powerful, unassailable, and dynamic.
- **Heart:** A personality that makes a person charismatic, clever, and attractive.
- **Club:** Something that feels powerful, alluring, or mysterious.
- **Diamond:** How something looks or feels fashionable, current, and exciting.

	Spade	Club	Heart	Diamond
A	Choose a word related to a profession, sport, art, or hobby that describes a moment of perfect mental competence.	Reference a creature or treasure famous for being difficult to catch.	Choose a word or phrase meaning "singular" or "unique."	Choose a word related to the most powerful force people in the setting understand.
K	Choose a word for a leader in an admired community.	Create a phrase that implies destruction.	Reference a person famous for being stylish and alluring.	Choose a word or phrase that implies something that cannot be contained or restricted.
Q	Choose a word for something invincible or indestructible.	Choose a word or create a phrase that implies something fictional but desirable.	Choose a word implying grace or poise.	Choose a word related to something old and timeless.

	Spade	Club	Heart	Diamond
J	Name a feature from an extremely useful piece of equipment.	Choose a word or create a phrase for something that cannot be touched.	Choose a word meaning "pleasant to touch."	Choose a word related to something new and revolutionary.
Even	Choose a word related to speed.	Choose a word related to darkness.	Choose a word related to light.	Choose a word related to color.
Odd	Choose a word related to extreme heat or cold.	Choose a word related to destruction.	Choose a word related to a pleasant sound.	Choose a word for something that no longer exists but is constantly referenced in art.
JR	A word that means something negative used as a positive.	A word that means something negative used as a positive.	A word that means something negative used as a positive.	A word that means something negative used as a positive.

Someone Bad

In a world focused on punks you need some sharp words people spit at each other in anger and resentment. These are insults and disparaging titles that different groups use to communicate; because anger is at the heart of punk you will need a lot of them. All of these words are derisive even if they have otherwise positive connotations.

SUITS AND COLORS

- **Red:** Prompts for words used by punks and revolutionaries to describe oppressors, compliant people, and unreliable allies.
- **Black:** Prompts for words used by oppressors and enforcers for dissidents, people they don't respect, and people who inconvenience them.

	Red	Black
A	A word for an unreachable place or thing	A word for someone who represents a credible threat to oppressors
K	A word for vulnerable authority figures with meaning related to "target" or "prey"	A word for dissident leaders implying structural importance like "keystone" or "axis"
Q	A word for someone untrustworthy with meaning related to "ambush"	A word implying someone is useless because they are a distraction
J	A word for someone who gives information to oppressors	A word for someone who can be broken and used as a tool
10	A word for an enforcer related to a machine capable of killing	A word for a difficult rebel derived from a word meaning "recurring error in a popular profession"

	Red	**Black**
9	A word for someone who resists oppressors in a way that creates risk for others with a meaning related to "unstable" or "toxic"	A word for a person protected by oppressing powers who is inconveniently off-limits to enforcers
8	A word for someone who talks about punk issues but behaves like an enforcer with a meaning related to "weapons" or "aggression"	A word for a group or activity that oppressors plan to shut down using a word based on "incarceration," "cancellation," or "execution"
7	A word for someone who poses as a punk but won't actually challenge enforcers with a meaning related to "weak" or "pretend"	A word for otherwise powerful people under the influence of oppressors with a meaning related to "asset" or "puppet"
6	A word for someone at the mercy of addictive substances that references death or loss	A word for someone at the mercy of addictive substances that references punishment
5	A word that appears complimentary or differential to oppressors but is actually an insult	A word for a member of the most influential body of enforcers referencing their power, danger, and disruptive nature
4	A word for enforcers with a meaning related to "disease," "decay," or "selfishness"	A word for a loved one who speaks against oppressors that references a historical event in the setting

	Red	Black
3	A word for an irritating person derived from a common inconvenience in a popular punk activity	A word for a victim of violence that will be covered up with a meaning related to "accident" or "mystery"
2	A word for someone completely lost to oppressor influence with a meaning related to "empty" or "broken"	A word for an expendable, nonthreatening, and compliant person with a meaning related to "object" or "acceptable loss"
JR	A word for someone who defects to oppressors	A word for a traitor to oppressors

Necessities

In addition to emphasizing what is good or bad, slang is a way cultures tend to identify what they value or consider taboo. These are prompts for ideas many cultures attach importance to, and will help you consider how people might discuss them in your world.

SUITS

- **Spade:** The prompts are related to the concept of skill or accomplishment. Punk worlds tend to focus on a few professions or activities that provide a frame for their ideas of accomplishment.
- **Club:** Almost every punk world has an important relationship with destruction. In a post-apocalyptic setting, ruin and decay are all around you; in a fascist dystopia, punks might yearn to mark the mask of their oppressors. Ideas that important need a variety of words.
- **Heart:** These prompts reference love and sex. They include both negative and positive implications that might fit different settings depending on their attitudes toward intimacy.
- **Diamond:** These prompts are related to the idea of value. Divisions of wealth and class are critical to many punk narratives. Defining the way different people discuss value helps build identity.

	Spade	**Club**	**Heart**	**Diamond**
A	A word tied to story or myth	A word referencing oblivion or insubstantial debris	A reference to loyalty or supplication	Something bright or reflective
K	A word meaning "precision" or "grace"	A word referencing age decay	A reference to infinity or eternity	Something new and untouched
Q	A word meaning "rare" or "unusual"	A word referencing reclamation or recycle	A reference to distant beauty or looming shadow	Something rare and pleasant, or old and exalted
J	A word meaning "excess" or "flourish"	A reference to a clean or skillful act of destruction	A reference to an ugly mark or alluring prize	Something useful that creates possibilities
Even	A word meaning "familiarity" or "casualness"	A word for a sight or sound that accompanies danger	A reference to connection or a tether	An abbreviation for something a character believes is universally valuable
Odd	A word implying frustration or disbelief	A word or phrase describing a common injury	A reference to movement or mess	A reference to measurements of valuable things

Making a Megacorp

Megacorporations, or megacorps, are companies that have grown into world-dominating goliaths. They have more resources than principles, and they aren't accountable to anyone. Their only goal is to grow as large as possible as quickly as possible by any means necessary, even if it causes conflict or comes at the expense of human life. They are a manifestation of misappropriated power and therefore perfect antagonists for punk.

Megacorps most frequently appear in cyberpunk, but they can be adapted to many subgenres. In steampunk a megacorps might run mines or factories; in dungeonpunk megacorps might recruit adventurers to risk their lives reclaiming artifacts; in apocalyptic punk megacorps might have ended the world.

This exercise will help you create a complicated and nefarious corporation for PCs to rage against. Most of these prompts are designed for a modern or futuristic setting, but the basic structure can be adapted to any punk world.

The Basics

The size of megacorporations generally makes the answer to the question "What does this company do?" pretty complicated. The point is unethical behavior, but they technically still need to offer goods or services.

To find your megacorps's core business model draw three cards from a standard deck of playing cards (with jokers included). The value of your cards will tell you this corporation's primary industries.

Black cards mean the corporation produces **goods** related to that industry like consumer products, vehicles, and productions. Red cards mean the corporation provides **services** related to that industry like managing workforces, institutional infrastructure, and utilities.

	Industry
A	Innovation [Draw another card; the corporation is developing something cutting edge for that industry.]
K	Weapons
Q	Medicine
J	Transportation
10	Banking
9	Engineering
8	Software
7	Manufacturing
6	Construction and real estate
5	Media
4	Food and agriculture
3	Utility management
2	Mining
JR	Front [Draw another card; that aspect of this corporation's business is a front for illegal activity.]

It's up to you to connect these ideas into a functional business model. Megacorps rarely start out as the monsters they become. Sometimes you start by building a search engine, and you end up developing advanced artificial intelligence. Look for connections anywhere you can find them.

Next choose **assets**, **threats**, and **corruptions** for your corporation. Assets make a corporation dominant in a market and dangerous to rivals. Threats are areas of weakness that can turn into major problems. Corruptions are serious moral failings that make a corporation dangerous to its employees and society at large.

Choose two from each category, never repeating a choice from a single row:

	Asset	Threat	Corruption
1	A charismatic CEO	Executives squabbling over an open leadership position	An incompetent or criminal CEO
2	A popular product	A product becoming outdated	A product dangerous to consumers
3	Valuable intellectual property	Intellectual property that will soon be worthless	Stolen intellectual property
4	Loyal and controlled employees	Fed up and organizing employees	Traitorous and negligent employees
5	Massive profits and unfathomable wealth	Debt and slowing growth	Embezzlement and internal looting
6	A good reputation and a popular brand	An unfolding scandal and an angry public	A brand built on hate and hostility

Now that you have an idea of this company's basic business and an understanding of their strengths and weaknesses, define three things they are known for. One product, one service, and one scandalous tragedy or crime they are responsible for.

📝 **Name three things this corporation is best known for:**

1. A specific product:

---

2. A specific service:

---

3. A tragedy or crime:

Now you have enough information to name this company. If you're having trouble thinking of something, draw two cards from a standard deck of playing cards (with jokers included) to find a prompt to create one. The name doesn't have to be "good." Most corporate names are created through committees and warped through mergers.

	First Half	Second Half
A	[Draw a new card and add a word like "Information," "Media," or "Digital" between that prompt and the second half]	[Take the root word and remove or change letters for an abbreviated homophonic version of itself]
K	[Any surname]	And Sons/and Daughters/and Family
Q	[Any city or location]	Institute
J	Black-/Dark-/[any noun that leads to a suitably ominous combination]	[A word thematically related to the industry like "life" for medical companies]

	First Half	**Second Half**
10	[Any word meaning "large"]	-Tech/Tech
9	[Any animal, mythological figure, or planet name]	-Safe/Secure/Sec/Securities
8	Data-/Info-/Digital	Bionics/Robotics/Genetics/Medical
7	Pod-/i-/e-/[any noun]	Horizons
6	[Surname] & [Surname]	Solutions
5	Imperial/Royal/Noble	-soft
4	Global/Planetary/Universe/Universal/Dimensional/Star/Sun	Inc/LLC/Corp/Industries/Enterprises
3	[Any random noun translated into a different language]	-dynamics/-dyne/-dine
2	[Any random noun]	[No second half]
JR	[An acronym that no longer stands for anything]	[Draw another card to combine with your first draw, then turn the result into an acronym]

Name:

Branding

A key tool in the arsenal of megacorporations is effective branding. Megacorps thrive when consumers don't see them for what they really are. However, they can only grow by doing things people don't like. The only way to maintain a positive reputation and continue to do terrible things is to control how a company's behavior is perceived.

With proper branding, bad behavior won't ever be noticed. In some cases you can even convince people to defend behavior they normally find morally abhorrent. It's all about how you position your message! Punks see through and subvert branding, but it allows megacorps to control the oppressed.

MESSAGING

You need to decide what your corporation wants people to see. If your corporation makes weapons, it's easy for folks to associate it with death and murder. However, if you associate your weapons with heroes who battle dangerous monsters, people will be more likely to think of action and adventure instead.

Name three things that your corporation wants to be associated with. These can be simple ideas like "strong" and "cool," goals like "innovation" and "progress," or outright lies like "safe" and "compassionate."

Brand associations:

You'll use these desired associations to help shape the look of brand messaging. As you create your logo and mascot, try to make connections to these core messages.

LOGO

A recognizable logo is how a brand quickly identifies its property and ties itself to specific ideas. Some corporations manage this really effectively and others miss the mark considerably.

To figure out your corporation's logo, roll two d6 to determine a style and how long they will have to go before changing it:

	Style	How Long Will It Last?
1	Obviously sinister imagery	This logo is ugly and problematic, but it will never change.
2	Just text, stylized calligraphy, or a letter	This is the third logo this year, and it won't last longer than the others.
3	A simple shape and color	This logo tries too hard to be trendy and current; it will only last a few years.
4	A complex abstract shape or pattern	This logo will be around for 5–10 years; it looks dated as soon as it changes because it is bound to a certain time.
5	Shape based on an object, animal, or person	This logo is the latest in a series of slight variations on a central theme. It will last 15–20 years before changing.
6	Roll twice and combine two styles	This logo has been in use almost as long as this company has existed; they have tried to change but always go back.

MASCOT

Sometimes you need to go further than a logo; some brands need a face. It's much easier to give traits to a character than to a company. A company named DarkCharge may make batteries that *allegedly* malfunction and explode, which is boring and bad! But DarkChaucer—the edgy DarkCharge mascot who rides a skateboard, raps, and uses energy weapons to blast people who try to sell him inferior batteries—is cool and good!

Mascots embody all the things you want your company to be. They can also stand in the line of fire when things go wrong. When and if DarkCharge loses customer respect, they can always rebrand DarkChaucer as "Chandler the safety-conscious lightning bug," a friendlier face for the newly named SafeSmart batteries.

Roll two d6 to generate a personality and a form for your megacorps mascot:

	Personality	Form
1	Misses their mark and is actually just creepy	Animal
2	Mildly antagonistic/Silly	Animal (anthropomorphized)
3	Friendly/Heroic	Person (cartoon or hologram)
4	Erudite/Parental	Person (cartoon hologram)
5	Glamorous/Sexy	Person (actual celebrity or company founder)
6	"Edgy" Cool	Existing fictional character or historical figure

Arms and Security

These are industries related to the manufacturing of arms, munitions, and the management of personnel for security and mercenaries for conflict. Profiteering off conflict and violence is practically a requirement for any megacorporation. Megacorps are so large they sometimes hold subsidiaries that seem to have nothing to do with their core business. Sales, mergers, and hostile takeovers can lead to a single company producing both your favorite sitcom and publishing your favorite author. To make things easy, we've broken down subsidiaries into seven industry categories, each with five potential businesses. Roll a d6 and select a number of subsidiary businesses for your megacorp equal to your result.

Subsidiaries
- Produces firearms and ammunition
- Produces combat vehicles
- Owns prisons or correctional facilities
- Operates a mercenary private military or police force
- Operates a mercenary intelligence firm

Media

The next evolution in advertising and outreach is fully controlling media platforms where consumers find your goods! Most of these options most easily fit modern and sci-fi settings. However, power over print and live performance is tremendously influential in historic settings.

Subsidiaries
- Owns a newspaper, news channel, and/or online information network
- Produces films, television, and/or live theater *or* publishes books, comics, and magazines
- Produces music entertainment including live performance and radio
- Operates a social media network and/or manages celebrities and "influencers"
- Creates games, theme parks, and interactive entertainment

Consumables

These are disposable goods that are used up or worn out and replaced. This is about capturing and creating necessities. Many of these relationships are born out of "vertical integration" and "synergy," like tobacco sellers expanding to manufacturing matches to dominate every part of the market. It's also about creating new ways to capitalize on established brands. Starting a war without selling T-shirts to honor the veterans of that war is leaving money on the table!

Subsidiaries

- Operates farms for meat and produce
- Produces processed foods and soft drinks
- Sells controlled substances like alcohol and tobacco
- Produces clothing, cosmetics, and lifestyle goods
- Produces consumable tools like matches, glue, or packaging

Medicine

This category involves any industry related to medicine and biological research. Having a medical division is key for understanding consumers inside and out. It's also much easier to cover up problems with your other businesses if *you* treat injuries your products cause. Every mistake represents a chance for potential profit!

Subsidiaries

- Operates hospitals and treatment clinics
- Produces medication and ongoing therapy and treatment
- Produces medical machines and equipment
- Runs schools, produces medical education materials, manages research and development
- Provides medical insurance and infrastructure

Utilities

This is any industry that manages essential services that make modern life possible. Managing a utility makes consumers truly dependent on your organization. Even if they hate everything about you, they can't live without you. Which is great!

Subsidiaries
- Mines fuel like oil, coal, and gas, or power production like nuclear, solar, or wind
- Operates telecom, cable, and Internet services
- Provides electricity or heat
- Provides water or sewage services
- Operates waste management or recycling services

Transportation

This is any business related to moving people and things from one place to another, anything from manufacturing vehicles, operating services, or managing a workforce. Everyone has to move stuff; doing your own transportation cuts out the middleman.

Subsidiaries
- Manufactures vehicles and parts for cars, trains, boats, aircraft, or spaceships
- Operates a mass transit system like trains, buses, or air travel
- Operates a specialty transit system like teleportation, hyperspace lanes, or a space elevator
- Operates a shipping and logistics service for transporting goods and resources
- Operates a transportation workforce supplying drivers, pilots, or delivery people

Finance

This is any business that manages money and property to turn it into more money and property. Megacorporations make absurd amounts of money, and if you don't operate your own bank, you're probably paying your competition.

Subsidiaries

- Holds assets like consumer and business checking and savings accounts, or operates vaults and storage facilities
- Provides personal or business loans
- Trades assets like stocks, mutual funds, or real estate
- Sells insurance or securities
- Produces and maintains a form of currency, either physical or digital

Held Together with Hope and Chewing Gum

Many punk stories follow characters who are constantly on the move, living in a single vehicle. This vehicle usually carries a few quirks that give it a sense of identity and even add to the tension of ongoing story lines. This exercise will help you create a vehicle that balances assets to help your PCs on their adventures; it should also include weaknesses that will make those adventures more interesting.

Assign priorities of 1 to 5 to your vehicle's **aggression**, **capability**, **reliability**, **comfort**, and **speed** without repeating a number. While most of these prompts might sound like they apply to a conventional land vehicle like a van or a truck, depending on your genre it could be a spaceship, mech suit, or even a living creature.

Aggression

In punk your PCs are likely to get into situations where they need more firepower than they can carry by hand. This need defines the combat capability of your vehicle, with a specific focus on weaponry.

1. This vehicle is some kind of legendary weapon. It allows you to take on opponents many times your size or maybe entire armies. Its destructive capabilities are almost terrifying. In the wrong hands this vehicle could cause a catastrophe with cosmic consequences.
2. In addition to an impressive array of standard armaments this vehicle is carrying something special: a weapon that can challenge opponents well outside this vehicle's class. It isn't something that can be used all the time due to limits on ammunition, power, or the vehicle's own structural integrity. This vehicle is a major threat in any combat, but people still probably underestimate it.
3. This vehicle has a standard array of defensive weapons for a vehicle in its class. In situations where you are outmatched it's probably best to retreat. However, you don't need to flinch from taking it into a fight either.
4. This vehicle has either minimal or no weapons. It's better served avoiding direct conflict. It probably has one offensive capability of any value, but it can only be used in extremely specific situations. It probably leaves the vehicle vulnerable after it is used.
5. This vehicle has absolutely no weapons. If you are taking it into a fight it's because you have no other options or you have made a huge mistake. The only advantage you carry is the ability to take a few hits before you make an escape.

Capability

This refers to functions of your vehicle outside of transportation and conflict. It's an extremely broad category that can cover the ability to seamlessly move between environments like land and water, specialized sensor arrays, and smuggling compartments.

1. This vehicle has a completely unique or experimental ability that nothing else in the universe is capable of. It is so capable that the full extent of its abilities are yet to be tested. Whenever the PCs are up against a wall, they can discover something new and unbelievable that this vehicle can do.

2. In addition to an array of standard functions, this ship has received special modifications that help you perform critical tasks more easily. It's full of after-market devices and special features that enable it to do work most other vehicles in its class would never be able to handle.

3. Mostly this is just a regular vehicle. However, it has one special modification or oddity that is useful in extremely specific situations.

4. All this vehicle can do is get you from point A to point B. Trying to use it for something else is like playing with fire. Even simple tasks like hauling a heavy load threaten to do serious damage.

5. You've actually had to dramatically cut down on the standard capabilities of this vehicle to accommodate other functions. Many of these functions are things people take for granted or essential capabilities that you have to bend over backward to compensate for lacking.

Reliability

Punks usually don't have access to the best equipment and have to work hard to keep moving. Lots of stories spring from needing repairs or extremely inconvenient mechanical troubles. You can also choose to take those problems off the table so your story can focus on other areas.

1. This vehicle is in some way invulnerable. It might be made out of a rare or mystic material, or it's just built with unparalleled craftsmanship. Whatever the cause, nothing apart from the driver's own actions can make this vehicle stop moving.
2. You almost never have to worry about this vehicle breaking down. It might not be indestructible, but it never lets you down. It has more tolerance for extreme conditions than pretty much everything else out there.
3. Part of this vehicle's function is to transport people in optimal conditions, allowing for a little rough weather. As long as you keep using it that way, you have nothing to worry about. If it has capabilities beyond that, you don't fully understand them or control them. It *might* be able to transform into an awesome robot, but you can't make that happen on a whim.
4. This vehicle has lots of quirks. Maybe you need to twist the ignition in just the right way to get the engine to turn over. Maybe you had to replace the wheel with a wrench. Most people wouldn't be able to turn this on, let alone drive it. It breaks down occasionally, but you can usually get things going as long as you're willing to add another quirk.
5. Every time you start this vehicle it might be the last time. It has been that way basically since the day you got it. For almost every trip you roll into a stop followed by an immediate breakdown. Emergency repairs while the vehicle is still moving probably aren't uncommon.

Comfort

Often in punk stories the vehicle used by the protagonists also acts as their home. This category determines how suited it is to that task and what sacrifices it demands of the group.

1. This vehicle is almost like a mobile spa. It is full of luxuries that make living in it a dream. It has everything anyone could want built in as a thoughtful and clever feature. No matter who hops aboard there is something waiting for them here. Even when the world outside is broken this place is a slice of heaven.

2. This vehicle is roomy and has comforts beyond any accepted standard. On top of all of the space and constructed comforts this vehicle has been given a personal touch through modification and decoration. It's not exactly a luxury experience, but it's easy to make a home in this place.

3. This vehicle can accommodate living space but it is very spare and utilitarian. There is just enough room to fit essential personal effects and there are certain luxuries that have to be sacrificed. However, everything people need to live is there, even if it's not pretty.

4. This vehicle was not made for many people to stay in it very long. It's definitely not made to be used the way your group has to. You're always having to sacrifice certain comforts to make it work. Sometimes it feels more like a prison than a vehicle.

5. No matter how many people there are in your party, this vehicle was made to support one fewer. Everything is cramped and you had to sacrifice a lot to make it that way. People are constantly arguing over space, and supplies have to be scarce.

Speed

One of the most essential questions about a vehicle is how fast it can go, especially when you spend a good deal of your time on the run from authority. How fast you go can be the difference between life and death.

1. This is literally the fastest vehicle of its type ever built. A lot of people say that as hyperbole; not your group. This was meticulously engineered to outrun anything in a race or a chase. Even if you think it's been pushed to its limit, it still has more to give.

2. This baby received custom modifications for speed. Nothing that rolls off a factory line could possibly match it. This vehicle might have competition from rigs run by gearheads obsessed with racing, but in most cases nothing gets past you.

3. This isn't fast, but it's not slow either. It was never built for racing so it won't ever be able to contend with the fastest vehicles out there. However, you don't need to be the fastest to stay ahead of what's after you; you just need to be fast enough.

4. Generally speaking it's slow. It *can* go fast, but it doesn't like to. Anytime you push this vehicle to move faster than a casual speed, you put it at risk. It might break down, or just set up a costly problem to address later. You have to choose when it's worth the trouble to move fast.

5. There is a problem that makes this vehicle move at a snail's pace. If you try to fix it, there are usually three more problems that pop up. There is no way to fix the speed without sacrificing something else critical. For now, when you pull into traffic, you slow everything down.

Neutral

There are too many RPG genres to ever address with one book. This final chapter has exercises to help you build concepts for just about any setting. Many of these will also work for the genres we addressed earlier in this book!

Big Bad

RPGs love a good confrontation with a villain. It might be a bit cliché, but there is something satisfying about finding a big bad evil guy pulling the strings behind the scenes, and then kicking their butt.

This exercise will help you quickly put your own spin on a classic idea. Assign priorities of 1 to 5 for this character's **cunning**, **strength**, **influence**, **plan**, and **corruption** without repeating a number. These qualities will come together to give you the perfect outline for your next Big Bad.

Cunning

This represents a villain's cleverness and intellectual assets. Intelligence is a complicated thing to quantify; it can manifest in many ways that make a villain an interesting threat. A cunning villain might be an accomplished scientist and engineer, military strategist, social manipulator, or combination of those traits. Prioritizing cunning makes a villain's mind one of their primary assets.

1. This villain is a once-in-many-generations intellect; they are almost impossible to outwit directly. They take care to understand both their enemies and their allies, almost never

underestimating their opposition or overestimating their own position. So long as they possess all the facts, they are extremely dangerous.

2. This villain is brilliant; they think tactically and strategically, considering every move their opponents make. However, they have a serious exploitable weakness. It might be that they depend too much on their plans and don't work well on their feet, or they may have become accustomed to underestimating their opponents because they are rarely challenged.

3. While they are no genius, this villain thinks in a very specific way that makes them dangerous. They are more cruel or willing to make sacrifices than other people, which makes them hard to predict and counter. This way of thinking also leads them into predictable or even compulsive patterns; PCs who understand those patterns should be able to find the upper hand.

4. This villain is not a gifted thinker, but they manage their resources well. If their operation has clever plans or makes strategic moves it is because they are following the advice of a wiser person. A clever PC can usually outwit them if they understand what the villain plans to do. Once a plan goes awry they are forced to withdraw or make critical mistakes.

5. This villain isn't clever, but they think they are. They attribute most of their past successes to their inherent superiority and constantly justify their opponents' successes as poor luck or unfair circumstances.

Strength

This represents a villain's prowess in battle. Some Big Bads need to be confronted with an army and team full of heroic PCs to be overcome; others need to be vanquished in one-on-one duels; and some can't fight at all. Prioritizing strength determines what kind of action you want to have in your climactic confrontation.

1. This villain is a cosmic threat. Either through physical strength, supernatural power, or individually controlled resources they are a threat to armies, planets, or even gods. There are very few beings who could match their might and almost none who are stronger.

2. This villain is undoubtedly one of the strongest beings in the setting. Alone they could challenge armies, monsters, and most heroes without worry. They need external assistance to challenge the strongest foes—depending on plans, minions, or equipment to maintain an advantage in epic struggles. They are a terrifying threat, but they are far from invincible.

3. This villain is very capable in a fight. Alone they can hold off groups and most skilled individuals with ease. They have to depend on external resources to challenge armies and conquer nations, but those goals are within their grasp. Working together, PCs are generally an even match for this villain in a direct conflict.

4. This villain is deadly only in very specific conditions. Perhaps they are an adept duelist, skilled pilot, master psychic, or talented magician. Their strength does not necessarily apply to all situations. They depend on external resources to overcome situations where they are outnumbered or pitted against certain skilled opponents. They have a clear advantage in one-on-one conflicts against PCs, but they would struggle to face down the full party.

5. This villain is not themselves a martial threat. They are either totally untrained in combat or they are contending with physical limitations—such as age or injury—that prevent them from fighting in the way they are accustomed. They require external resources to be a threat in a fight at all. Even a single PC should be enough to outmatch this villain in most circumstances.

Influence

Some villains menace the world through their ability to command people and resources. The more you prioritize influence for a Big Bad, the less your PCs will confront them directly in your story. An army of minions and subordinates allows PCs to win battles without making the Big Bad appear weak. Influence also helps motivate the PCs to act because a villain with considerable resources can easily overcome traditional institutional justice.

1. This villain has all but absolute control over the world. They are less concerned with acquiring power than they are with maintaining power. Any imaginable resource that could be mustered against an enemy is already within their grasp, and they may even be able to command powers that no one else in the setting could possibly understand.

2. Not only does this villain command the most formidable mundane resources in the setting like armies, corporations, and political authority; they can also use those resources to do things that would be impossible for anyone else. This allows them to develop new technology, uncover ancient secrets, and otherwise give themselves power no one else is able to possess.

3. This villain has a great deal of influence in terms of societal authority and wealth. They might command a small nation, massive corporation, clandestine organization, or some combination thereof. They may have to contend with legal and diplomatic restrictions to their power, but with work those can be circumvented.

4. This villain can put pressure on many powerful people. They either control a modest organization outright, have a good deal of authority over a large one, or command a fanatic cult of personality. It is difficult for them to openly exercise their power without drawing the wrath of the law or political rivals—but there is plenty they can do behind the scenes.

5. This villain either works alone or with just a handful of followers. Through wealth or skill they have access to enough resources to keep themselves dangerous, but capturing anything significant requires work, planning, and leverage.

Plan

This represents the threat posed by a villain's central strategy. A plan can be a web of political influence backing a destructive agenda, a carefully managed military campaign, an opportunity to seize and use a MacGuffin, or vague ideas haphazardly strung together. A good plan doesn't necessitate a clever villain; even a foolish person with the right opportunity can pose a huge threat. Highly prioritized plans might present a threat even if the Big Bad is captured or killed.

1. This villain's plan is built into a complex web of interconnecting forces. It takes several tedious conversations just to make someone understand how these elements are connected and what makes that dangerous—let alone identify how the Big Bad is behind it. It is difficult to identify a central goal even for an informed person. There are so many contingencies and countermeasures that thwarting one move feels like playing into another.

2. The villain's plans are for a time aligned with the PC's goals and actions. Through careful investigation it is possible to see the agenda the villain is pushing forward. Once certain aspects are in motion they will be very difficult to halt, and it will take real effort to convince someone of the truth even after you point it out.

3. The villain's plan is straightforward and involves a simple, attainable goal. It is easy to understand their goals and why those goals might be dangerous. It's likely that this plan already has many essential elements in place and it is bound to succeed if left unopposed. There are multiple paths to success, and the plan can suffer setbacks without falling apart.

4. This villain's plan is:
    1. A flawless piece of art with intricate, delicate components. If left unopposed it will surely succeed, but it will crumble with opposition.
    2. Not well thought out but relying upon such stable resources that it still poses a credible threat.

3. More of a series of loosely interconnected actions based on a theme or ideology. There is no end goal beyond sending a message. The plan is difficult to thwart because it isn't really aiming for one thing.
5. This villain doesn't appear to really have a plan at all. Their operation seems to revolve around hubris and presumed weakness in their enemies, or they are depending on fundamentally uncontrollable forces. Even unopposed they might thwart themselves part of the time.

Corruption

This represents how irredeemable a villain is and what it might take to stop them from pursuing destructive action. A truly corrupt villain will pursue their ideology undaunted by any sacrifice or negative consequences; villains who are less corrupt may be defeated before they are destroyed. This shapes the options PCs have to overcome or even save the Big Bad from themselves.

1. This villain is the embodiment of their ideology. They might literally be the avatar of an abstract concept, or they have shaped their mind so firmly around an ideal it is impossible to sway them from their path. They will be utterly defeated or destroyed before they are swayed from their path.
2. This villain is a fanatic devotee of a toxic worldview or philosophy. They will not stray from their path without a truly profound moment of epiphany. Simple negotiation or pleas for reason will not have an effect.
3. This villain is selfish, callous, and opportunistic. They commit acts of evil not because of ideology, but because they don't care that what they are doing is wrong and they believe no one will stop them. They can be swayed and blocked in many instances, but it would take a fundamental re-education to pull them from their path.
4. This villain acts primarily from a place of hurt and trauma. Their motivations and goals are sympathetic but they are willing to

hurt others in order to reach them. They might even be aware of hypocrisy in their actions but embrace them nonetheless through nihilistic cynicism. It is possible to negotiate or sway this villain toward a path of redemption, but you will have to overcome their disdain for moderate platitudes.

5. This villain perpetrates acts of evil because they have misplaced their faith in a corrupt system. They might have sympathetic goals or motivations, but they continually invest their efforts poorly. Negotiating with them will be frustrating, as they will probably agree with the PCs on a fundamental level but insist that the solution requires a deeper dedication to harmful actions.

Impregnable, Except...

Powerful superweapons and impenetrable fortresses make excellent set pieces for climactic action. They give protagonists something emblematic of the villain's diabolical power to heroically stand against.

It's possible to go too far when building a superweapon to the point you undermine its role in the story. Superweapons exist to be destroyed. If they are *actually* indestructible there is no point in standing against them. If you want to see the heroes save the day you are better off establishing weaknesses and vulnerabilities alongside strengths when setting the stage for your dramatic final conflict.

☀ **Choose two vulnerabilities for every strength your superweapon or fortress possesses:**

○ It's Extremely Well Defended
- The guards are easy to impersonate.
- They don't understand where their true vulnerability lies.
- Security protocols can easily be manipulated.
- It also holds prisoners or other people who would be sympathetic to your cause.
- There is a time where those defenses are unavoidably weaker.
- The ability of guards is conditional based on equipment or forces that they don't fully control.

- It's Difficult to Find
  - Its hiding place also makes it very difficult to flee an attack.
  - That means they are not anticipating an attack.
  - It is located far from reinforcements.
  - It will have difficulty signaling for help.
  - The terrain surrounding it is better understood by people who want to destroy it than the people who want to defend it.
  - It is not self-sufficient and depends on external supply runs.

- It's Resistant to Ordinary Weapons
  - Except in locations they won't think to defend.
  - But not the extraordinary weapons you plan to attack with.
  - Which means they focused less on defending the inside with personnel and security.
  - It is very difficult to repair.
  - That resistance depends on a shield that can be disabled.
  - But only on the outside.

- It Has Untold Destructive Power
  - It needs time to charge or prepare its signature weapon.
  - That power is experimental and open to failure.
  - It requires a rare and volatile resource to work.
  - It can only focus on one target at a time.
  - It becomes vulnerable when active.
  - It can only be active for a short period of time.

- It Is Mobile
  - It can only move over certain terrain.
  - It becomes vulnerable to attack either right before or right after moving.

- Each movement requires precise calculation, charging, or some other time-consuming logistical process.
- It can travel in straight lines but struggles to maneuver and course correct.
- It draws resources away from critical destructive power.

The Prize

One of the easiest ways to get PCs going is to dangle an appetizing prize in front of them. A big pile of treasure generally does the trick, but considering different dimensions of a prize challenges PCs in new ways and leads to more interesting stories. Varied rewards also help each adventure feel distinct.

There are lots of factors that make things valuable. Some casks of whiskey recovered from shipwrecks sell for thousands of dollars an ounce, movie memorabilia sells for millions, and billions are spent on bad investments chasing something impossible. A good prize becomes valuable through a combination of factors; once you understand how much each aspect influences your prize, you can fill in the blanks to make something special.

For this exercise you'll define the **rarity**, **utility**, **tradeability**, **mobility**, and **notoriety** for a prize using the priority system. Assign priorities of 1 to 5 for each quality without repeating a number.

Rarity

Things that are hard to find and acquire have straightforward value. For PCs there is another interesting dynamic at play: "How hard is it for me to encounter this in the story?" For protagonists, encountering unusual things is more a question of "when" than "if." When determining rarity consider opportunity as a factor alongside availability and uniqueness.

1. This prize is singular. There is nothing like it anywhere else in the universe. It might be the product of a unique historical event, an aspect of a remarkable being, the design of a rare intelligence, or a precious heirloom from a PC's family. If you don't claim it there will never be another chance like this again.
2. This prize is extraordinary; there are only a handful of things like it anywhere in the world. Maybe it is a part of a rare collection, a prototype in a line of experimental goods, a possession of an important historical figure, or a personal piece of a PC's history. Unless you dedicate your life to searching, it is unlikely you'll find something like this again.
3. This is as rare as gold. It might be hard to find, hard to make, something everyone wants, or a common good collected in a way that is remarkably convenient—in any case, you almost always have to work or be very lucky to get your hands on something like this. Even if you will probably see something like this again, this is a good deal.
4. The only thing rare about this prize is the amount available or something slightly quirky about its format. It could be a large amount of a common resource, or a common good being moved in a significant way. You don't necessarily see something like this every day, but the commodity isn't exactly rare.
5. There is very little unusual about this prize. That doesn't mean it's useless, but its value doesn't come from being difficult to find.

Utility

Value also comes from practicality. PCs define themselves through action, so utility is a great incentive for a prize. In a post-apocalyptic world bullets and water might be more valuable than gold simply because they have a more immediate use. In many cases a fully functional mech suit is just more interesting than a fat stack of credits, even if those credits could buy you a mech suit.

1. This prize provides you with a completely unique opportunity impossible to come by from other means. It could be related to the resource the prize is composed of, a personal attachment a notable figure has to the prize, or timing surrounding how you find it. This prize will let you do something you could never dream of in a thousand years.
2. Even completely divorced from monetary value, this prize is incredibly useful. As raw material it could permanently enhance your equipment; it could be a tool like a remarkable weapon or vehicle; or it could even be information in an ancient tome or computer file. Whatever this prize is, the PCs have the potential to use it for themselves to incredible effect.
3. This prize is useful, but it might require the PCs to change their plans or adapt their lifestyles. Depending on how far out of their way they're willing to go it could still be an asset. No matter what, its utility makes it valuable to someone.
4. If this prize is valuable for utility, it's valuable to an extremely narrow demographic of people. This prize still technically works, but it's either outdated or meant for an esoteric purpose. Alternatively, its utility could be very generic, like allowing you to exchange it for something you really want.
5. This prize is not practical in any way. If it was a tool or practical resource at any point that was in the long-ago past. Now it exists only to be admired and coveted.

Tradeability

After getting a prize the PCs can have a full adventure just trying to get rid of it. A briefcase full of illegal weapons might be worth millions, but selling them means dealing with the most dangerous criminals in the world while avoiding the authorities—almost more trouble than value. When creating a prize, consider how much you want to think about what comes next.

1. It is easy to safely and securely contact buyers and sell this prize. It takes almost no effort to list its sale, there are plenty of buyers, and there is no legal risk.
2. There are some risks involved in moving a prize like this, but they are not really a consideration if you use common sense. There are a decent number of interested buyers and a few marketplaces set up to move goods like this, but you might have to look for them.
3. Selling a prize like this will be a bit of a chore. It could be that these goods are illegal and you will need to go out of your way to find a buyer, or the challenge could be a high price or niche demand. No matter what, you are going to have to do some legwork if you intend to sell it, and if you aren't careful there could be serious consequences.
4. Selling a prize like this is an incredibly dangerous and difficult process. There are no established markets for this sort of thing even from illegitimate sources. In most cases you will have to locate and contact buyers directly, and you'll have to worry about law enforcement through the entire process.
5. This prize is almost impossible to sell. Every conceivable obstacle will stand in your way. If something goes wrong, losing the value of the prize will be the least of your concerns. It will be as much trouble to move this prize as it was to take it, if not more.

Mobility

Not all prizes are suited to sleight of hand or smash and grab. Sometimes the most difficult part of the operation is moving the prize from one place to another. Sometimes you can't really move what you are trying to claim at all. Mobility helps determine where the challenge lies in claiming a prize and has a big influence on what the prize looks like.

1. This prize is almost weightless, practically invisible, and easy to secure. A single person can move the prize without anyone noticing. Data is a great fit for this sort of prize, but it also works with jewelry, magic artifacts, nanomachines, and all sorts of other small and valuable packages.
2. This prize requires a strong person, a team of people, or standard vehicles to move. Picture something that could be loaded into a car, wagon, or van. With careful planning it can move pretty freely, but it's not devoid of risk.
3. To even think about moving a prize like this, PCs will have to do some work hunting down specialty vehicles and equipment. This prize requires large industrial vehicles, containment equipment, or monitoring to move securely. It is still possible to get from one place to another; it just takes a lot of work.
4. This prize is not mobile in a traditional sense. A mine is a perfect example of this sort of prize; you can absolutely move what people find valuable, but it requires a complex operation and lots of specialty equipment and expertise.
5. This prize cannot be moved. It's most likely a fixed place that holds value like a castle, planet, or dimension. Having access to this prize is still incredibly valuable, but it's not the sort of value you can ever take with you.

Notoriety

While there are definitely prizes that wear their value on their sleeve, some are followed by legends and rumors that make them infinitely more desirable. Notoriety can also have an impact on how easy it is to hold on to or sell a prize. Whether it's adding value, causing problems, or a combination of the two, notoriety is absolutely something to consider when making a compelling prize.

1. This prize is a household name in many places, and if people see it there is a very good chance they will know what it is. Almost everyone finds some novelty in the prestige of owning or interacting with it, even if they don't have a use for it.
2. There is a history behind this prize; in the right circles it will raise eyebrows. Perhaps it was created by an influential artist or celebrity, or the prize itself was involved in a significant historical event. Even if the majority of people wouldn't know just by looking, this prize holds an allure beyond function or rarity.
3. The actual prize has a reputation, but people traveling with this sort of thing also carry a stigma. If folks know your PCs have this prize they will be treated differently. That can be good or bad depending on whom they encounter.
4. This prize won't attract too much attention. That's a blessing if you are just trying to get it from one place to another, but it might be a problem if you're trying to sell it as something special.
5. This prize has an extremely bad reputation; everyone knows what it is and they believe it is extremely cursed. You might meet a few weirdos who have an interest in it, but they would definitely be dangerous weirdos.

Five Battles

Conflicts shape history. Even media covering current events tend to present stories in terms of disagreements. This structure is a handy tool for defining a new place and understanding the people who live there. Use the following prompts to understand the five battles that define a location and how they affected the community.

Something Terrible

This place was affected by a war or massive calamity. It happened generations ago, so only the oldest people have firsthand knowledge of it. Education and culture were significantly impacted by this conflict, but it happened so long ago that most people can't imagine living any other way. It left an artifact behind—a building or a monument.

✏ **What change did people accept to recover from this event?**

✏ **What does the artifact look like?**

Something Political

A pivotal political conflict was settled a few years ago. It's still fresh in the memory of people involved. People continue to define themselves by how they saw the issue.

✏ **Did this battle cause change, prevent change, or define change?**

✏ **How has the losing side suffered? Will future generations identify with their suffering?**

Something Periodic

This community always returns to a familiar battle, a thing of pride and joy, and everyone seems invested in a certain outcome. This battle probably occurs once every year or so.

✎ **How are victors of this battle honored?**

✎ **How do people signify which champion they support?**

Something Tender

There is a tension that lies just below the surface of this community. It works its way into the hearts of everyone—even those who wish to remain out of it. This issue is waiting to boil over into something much uglier.

✎ **When do people talk about it?**

✎ **What, if any, efforts to resolve it resulted in escalation?**

Something Petty

This is a conflict that most people in the community observe but do not participate in directly. It plays out through absurd actions that always go too far.

✎ **What is broken because of this conflict?**

✎ **What hapless victims are caught in the middle?**

The Bar

One of the most important set pieces in an RPG story is a bar. Whether you call it a tavern, inn, saloon, pub, roadhouse, or café— these places are essential for any group of heroes. A bar can be a base of operations, a source of information, a neutral location to conduct business, or a place to celebrate victory with a meal and a drink.

This exercise will help you quickly create a bar with a sense of character with options for multiple settings.

The Inns and Outs

To get started choose set priorities for your bar's **discretion**, **loyalty**, **connections**, **information**, and **service** from 1 to 5 without repeating a number.

DISCRETION

Sometimes you need to go where *nobody* knows your name. PCs tend to lead rebellions, pull heists, and commit other off-the-books deeds to support their heroics. A bar that can keep a secret is vital.

1. This place prides itself on privacy and anonymity. The location itself is secret, requiring a password or special knowledge to get in. It might even move around. There are private places to conduct business, a dress code to conceal identity, and fail-safes in case of a leak. If you can't keep a secret here, it's not safe anywhere.
2. Only the most resourceful information brokers can get hints at deals struck here. There are secluded spaces to meet and the staff don't talk about your business, as long as you remember to tip.
3. The layout of this place is baffling. There always seems to be more dark corners than patrons. There are no special policies in place to protect the clientele, but mostly people mind their own business.
4. Eavesdropping and gossip are practically a sport for the regulars here. In fact, sitting down almost guarantees that someone will eventually come over and get involved in your conversation.

5. This place is run by a powerful and influential organization. They see and hear everything that happens here. Anything that hides in this place has to do so in plain sight.

LOYALTY

There's a difference between being a patron, a regular, and a friend. In the world of an RPG, that difference can mean the difference between life and death.

1. The owner owes the PCs, big time. Maybe they saved the owner's life, or introduced them to their one true love. Whatever the reason, the owner would take any imaginable risk to keep the PCs safe.
2. At least one of the PCs is old friends with management. They'll always take the party's side in a conflict and even stick their necks out to provide an alibi. There are practical limits to this loyalty, but if used judiciously this is an invaluable resource.
3. Perhaps the PCs have been regular customers for years, the owner has a crush, or the management just respects their profession. The party is treated well so long as they don't bring in too much trouble. Even if there is a little problem, management can probably be convinced to look the other way.
4. As long as you've got money, you'll be treated like everyone else. If you make trouble, everything costs more money. Once your pockets are empty you're out the door.
5. Management doesn't like one or all of the PCs. They'll tolerate their presence as long as the party pays. However, given an opportunity they will sell the group out or create a problem for them.

CONNECTIONS

Bars attract all sorts of clients. If you go to the right place you might be sitting next to the world's greatest assassin or the overworked assistant to the high-ranking executive. Every place has a different atmosphere; it just depends on whether you're aiming high or low.

1. Some of the most important people in the world go out of their way to have a drink here. Heroes, political leaders, supernatural beings, and other celebrities will always stop by given the chance. When you need a miraculous and improbable meeting, this is where you go.

2. The wealthy and powerful choose to gather here behind the scenes. It's a place where masks come off and deals get struck. If you need to find someone with ties to the upper echelons of society, you can find them here.

3. This place will surprise you. Someone here might be able to help you get a hundred gallons of holy water pretty cheap, a rare out-of-print book, or a list of people to bribe to get into a secure location.

4. This place is frequented by working folks; regulars include security guards, union workers, petty criminals, and minor heroes from a bygone age. There probably isn't a ton of direct power, but there's a wealth of knowledge and experience that might point you in a good direction.

5. This bar is home to the seediest corners of the underworld. Everyone here would kill you for a nickel and then use that nickel to put a hit on their grandmother. Some patrons are heads of organized crime, legendary assassins, or supervillains. If you need to do the worst things imaginable, you can get started by coming here.

INFORMATION

Adventures always need incredibly specific information. The easiest place to start a hunt for any kind of information is a bar. The information you get is entirely dependent on the type of place it is.

1. There is someone here who has been waiting for years to deliver an extremely critical piece of information to a group exactly like the PCs. It is a slice of destiny that the party couldn't find anywhere else.

2. Someone here likes to keep tabs on things happening in the area and the world in general. They also make it their business to pass on what they know. It might be something they do out of a sense of moral obligation, to satisfy feelings of self-importance, or to make some extra coin. No matter the reasoning it means that PCs can usually find what they are looking for.

3. This place is home to a group with very specific expertise. They might be veterans, scientists, or historians. If PCs look, they can find people who know too much about weirdly specific stuff.

4. Either the bar or its patrons consider it a major faux pas to talk about other people's business. You'll probably get into trouble looking for information here.

5. This place is full of very convincing liars who make their livings by selling stories that sound very close to legitimate information. It's very difficult to tell what is fact and what is fiction here.

SERVICE

Sometimes you need to know how good your bar is at being a bar. The kind of food and drink a bar serves helps establish character. It also says a lot about the people who go there.

1. This place is special in one very specific area. Perhaps the food is prepared by an underappreciated master chef, the bar is stocked with impossibly rare spirits, world-class musicians

compete to provide the entertainment, or the walls are covered in spectacular works of art. It's got one thing that is so special it doesn't exist anywhere else.

2. Everything is tailored to please refined palates. The food and drink are expensive and rare. The decoration and atmosphere are either opulent to the point of being gaudy, or engineered to the point of being soulless. This place was designed to make even the social elite feel as though they are out of their league.

3. This place is down to earth and homey. The food and drink invite nostalgia. The decoration and atmosphere are comfortable and familiar. If there is entertainment you are sure to hear your favorite songs. Everything about this place is cheap, but it's cheap in all the right ways.

4. This place is either utterly unremarkable or so avant-garde that it's impossible to enjoy. The food could be overly processed and bland corporate mush, or what should be simple dishes tortuously reconstructed through molecular gastronomy. There are taps of flavorless light beer or bizarre high-concept cocktails. The music is a single droning pop song that lost its charm weeks ago, or operatic noisecore covers of that same song. Everything is either bad from lack of trying or bad from trying far too hard.

5. This place is absolutely filthy. All the drinks are watered down, all the food is cold, and every surface feels sticky. Despite the low quality it feels like you are paying just a little bit too much for what you're getting—not enough to make you leave, but enough to annoy you. If you had other options, you probably wouldn't be here.

Name

Nothing is worse than panic-naming something that sticks around for a whole campaign. To generate something that fits, just choose the most appropriate genre from the table, then draw two cards from a standard deck (jokers included).

Fantasy		
	First Half	**Second Half**
A	[Any god]'s	Kiss
K	The Crowned	Dragon
Q	Her/His/Their Majesty's	Spell/Enchantment
J	The [A compliment one might give a prince or princess]	Chest/Hoard
10	The [Any monster]'s	[Any jewelry or clothing]
9	The [Any stone]	Hearth/Fire
8	The Widow's	Blade/Sword/Bow
7	[Any animal]'s	[Any instrument]
6	The Burning	Axe/Hatchet/Knife
5	The Witch's/Wizard's/ Necromancer's	Tap/Cask
4	The [Any color]	Inn/Tavern
3	Two [Any tree]'s	Stein/Goblet
2	The Broken/Leaking/Mended	Trough/Bucket
JR	The [Any insult]	Puddle/Stain

	Noir	
	First Half	**Second Half**
A	[This bar has no name]	The bar's location
K	Bogey/Cagney/Lorre/Payne/ Mitchum/Orson's	[A euphemism for death]
Q	Bacall/Stanwyck/Lake/Davis/ Crawford/Bennett/De Carlo's	Dream
J	The [Anything delicate]	[A euphemism for jail]
10	[Any first name popular in the 1940s]	Kiss
9	The [Any expression about rain like "Pouring" or "Cats & Dogs"]	Club
8	The Sweet Sorrow/Farewell	Jungle
7	The [Any flower]	Heat
6	The Starlight/Moonlight	Place/Room
5	The [Any building material used in an urban environment]	Café
4	The Midnight	Jazz Room
3	The Sunset/Twilight	Riverside
2	The [Any gambling terminology]	Goodbye
JR	Draw another card and select a prompt from the first half list; that's the whole name	Draw another card; its suit or value is the second half of the name

	First Half	Second Half
Western		
A	The [Any frontier or desert animal]	Draw another card for your second half and add "and Show"
K	[Any slang for alcohol]	Saloon
Q	The [Any Western word for authority like "Ranger" or "Sheriff"]'s	[Any equipment used with horses]
J	[Any Western slang for criminal like "Outlaw" or "Rustler"]'s	Hideaway/Hideout/Escape
10	The Last/Far Out/Land's End	Refuge
9	[Any word for a rock formation]	Trading Post
8	[The] Big Sky/Star/Moon	Cantina/Canteen
7	[The] Fireside/The Sunrise	Oasis
6	[The] [Any poker result]	Corral
5	[The] Gunsmoke	Inn
4	[The] [Any instrument]	Sunset
3	(The) Tumbleweed/Cactus Flower	Creek
2	Roughneck/Roughrider	Trough
JR	[Any Western-sounding first name]	[Any word for where an animal lives]

Sci-Fi (Cyberpunk/Near Future)		
	First Half	**Second Half**
A	[Any sci-fi author] (optional: 's)	[Replace any letters in the first half with numbers and symbols]
K	Macro/Micro/Giga/Nano	[Pull a second half from the fantasy list]
Q	[Any periodic element]	Diner/Eatery
J	Digital/Cyber	Torrent
10	i/e	Brought to you by [any megacorps]
9	Fractal	Bit/Byte/Bite
8	Liquid/Drink	[Any computing suffix like .exe/.com/.jpeg]
7	Corrupted	//drink
6	Frag/Defrag	[Any business jargon]
5	Pixel/Polygon	Flames/Fire
4	Glitch	Override/Matrix
3	Neon/Neo	Virus/Crash
2	[Any meme]	[Any fast casual restaurant]
JR	[No first half]	[No second half]

Sci-Fi (Space)		
	First Half	**Second Half**
A	[Any astronaut or physicist's surname]'s	Black Hole (optional: Add an article before the first half)
K	[Any nonsense alien name]'s	Thrust/Boost/Pulse
Q	[Any periodic element]	Splendor
J	[Any mythological figure]'s	Cantina/Saloon/Diner/Pub
10	Astro/Cosmo/Cosmic	Dimension/Galaxy
9	[Any Western-sounding word]	Port/Station
8	Comet/Meteor	Nebula/Nova
7	Binary/Elliptical	Star/Sun/Moon/Planet
6	Penumbra/Umbra	[Any weather event]
5	Quantum/Quasar	[Any number]
4	Gravity's	Ring/Belt/Field
3	Orbital/Magnetic	[Any hostile environment]
2	Control/Directive	[Any first name that sounds way too normal]
JR	[Any food or drink item]	[Any result from the fantasy list]

Patrons

Finally, bars need NPCs. If there is a chance your group is going to talk to someone, they should make the story interesting. This table will help you generate an NPC based on how they feel about your PCs.

We've broken down NPC attitudes toward PCs into four categories:

1. **Friendly:** This person feels good about your PCs, is just nice in general, or happens to need the help from folks like your PCs.
2. **Unfriendly:** They either don't like your PCs or they are generally looking to cause trouble.
3. **Hapless:** This person makes a perfect victim for your party to frustrate or for temptation to lure them into trouble.
4. **Mysterious:** This person carries an air of mystery or serendipity that can pull your party into external intrigue.

Draw a card from a standard deck of playing cards (jokers included) and match its suit and value to the following chart. If you already know what attitude you want your patron to have toward the PCs, feel free to ignore the suit.

	Friendly [Hearts]	Unfriendly [Spades]	Hapless [Clubs]	Mysterious [Diamonds]
A	An old friend who owes one of the PCs a favor	An agent of one of the primary antagonists currently in disguise	An extremely powerful and important person traveling in disguise	Someone who is typically antagonistic to the PCs who feels conflicted about their place in the world

	Friendly [Hearts]	Unfriendly [Spades]	Hapless [Clubs]	Mysterious [Diamonds]
K	Someone the PCs have inadvertently helped in the course of their adventures	Someone the PCs have inadvertently hurt in the course of their adventures	Someone on an extremely important and delicate assignment who cannot afford interference	Someone who will inadvertently help or hinder the PCs in a major way while the PCs are in the bar
Q	An old flame for one of the PCs that they still have a good relationship with despite a complicated history	Either a jilted ex-lover of one of the PCs or someone looking to seduce one of them for an ulterior motive	Someone with a harmless infatuation with one of the PCs	An attractive stranger who is an uncanny match for one of the PCs
J	A friendly rival who is easily goaded into absurd contests	An antagonistic rival who has a history of goading one of the PCs into absurd contests	A person who is extremely accomplished in a field that is important to one of the PCs	A wandering savant who has mastered a skill that is coincidentally useful to one of the PCs

	Friendly [Hearts]	Unfriendly [Spades]	Hapless [Clubs]	Mysterious [Diamonds]
10	Someone who has heard of the exploits of one or more of the PCs and is a fan of their heroism	Someone who has been spreading inaccurate and negative stories about the PCs	Someone who is terrified of the PCs because of technically accurate but slightly skewed stories they have heard	Someone with a useful story relating to the backstory of one of the PCs or primary antagonists
9	An older person with lots of experience and wisdom who is looking to help folks	A cynical person looking to tempt one of the PCs from a healthy path, or wishes to challenge one of the PC's deeply held beliefs	An older person who can't help but be inconvenienced by the PCs	An older person who says something cryptic that could be useful to the PCs, but they never explain what their words mean
8	A businessperson who is looking to make a deal with a group like the PCs	A swindler who is looking for targets like the PCs	A person with something valuable the PCs need, but they don't want to part with it	A person selling strange and intriguing goods that coincidentally will be very useful to the PCs

	Friendly [Hearts]	Unfriendly [Spades]	Hapless [Clubs]	Mysterious [Diamonds]
7	A group of rowdy locals who are deeply amused by one of the PCs	An angry rabble of locals who have a bone to pick with the PCs	A group of incredibly proper people who are easily offended	A clandestine organization trying very hard not to be noticed
6	A competent patron looking to make a good-natured wager over a contest of skill	A cunning skill shark looking to dupe a mark with a wager over a contest	A foolish person looking to make wagers they probably shouldn't	A person offering rewards for seemingly simple concepts
5	Someone who shares a cultural tie to one of the PCs	Someone who has unfavorable views toward a profession or culture belonging to one of the PCs	A person who has a cultural background that makes them of extreme interest to one or more of the PCs	A person who has a cultural background or profession that the PCs believed to be mythical or extinct

	Friendly [Hearts]	Unfriendly [Spades]	Hapless [Clubs]	Mysterious [Diamonds]
4	Someone celebrating a bit of good news	Someone who has suffered a recent tragedy	Someone who will suffer a terrible tragedy in the bar while the PCs are present	Someone who will learn a bit of good news in the bar while the PCs are present
3	A well-meaning traveler who is both extremely naive and extremely sweet	A loud-mouthed braggart with more money than sense and more pride than skill	A pitiable sad sack who cannot help but suffer amusing misfortunes	Someone who looks incredibly distinct and out of place to such a degree it's easy to assume they are important
2	A chatty drunk who can't seem to leave the party alone	A know-it-all jerk who constantly interjects to correct or dismiss people	Someone who can't help but accidentally reveal valuable information that they would like to keep secret	Someone who seems to know far too much about the PCs

	Friendly [Hearts]	Unfriendly [Spades]	Hapless [Clubs]	Mysterious [Diamonds]
JR	A supernatural or mythic being in disguise and with a desire to help the PCs	A supernatural or mythic being in disguise who wants to settle a petty score with one of the PCs	A supernatural or mythic being in disguise who is just trying to have a quiet night	A supernatural or mythic being in disguise who wants to make some trouble for fun

We Built This City (on Talk and Rolls)

Every city is a world in its own right. They develop customs, landscapes, and languages that someone could spend a lifetime studying. That makes them a wicked problem for worldbuilding, especially in RPGs. PCs can pack years of adventure into a few square blocks, or visit a marvelous metropolis for a day before moving on to discover something new.

This exercise will help you make an outline for a city with a distinct character that will fit in almost any genre. Then you will populate it with iconic **landmarks**, **residents**, and **events or rumors** to ensure your PCs will always remember it.

Basics

A city can mean a thousand different things. Chicago, Venice, and Las Vegas are all cities, but they look and feel very different. Their **population**, **shape**, **age**, and **wealth** helped them develop unique traits.

Choose or roll on the following tables to find the traits that shape your city.

POPULATION

To make a city you need a rough idea of how many people live in it. Numbers won't really tell you anything; in fiction big cities can have hundreds to trillions of residents. Instead, focus on how large that population is compared to other places in the world, and the physical space the city occupies.

 Roll a d4 or choose one:

1. (1 Eccentricity or 1 Asset)
2. (1 Asset)
3. (1 Asset or 1 Corruption)
4. (1 Corruption)

1. **Large:** This city has one of the densest populations in the world. There are many special adaptations that allow it to accommodate so many.
2. **Medium:** This city is home to millions of people without functioning too differently from the rest of the world.
3. **Small:** This city holds less than a million people. It is larger than most of the towns nearby, but it holds little significance on a world stage.
4. **Spare:** This city is actually underpopulated for the resources and infrastructure it holds.

SHAPE

After population, most people look to physical size as a characteristic for cities. The amount of space a city takes up is less important than how that space is used. The shape of your city says a lot about how people live in it.

 Roll a d4 or choose one:

1. (1 Corruption)
2. (1 Eccentricity)
3. (1 Asset)
4. (1 Eccentricity or 1 Corruption)

1. **Sprawling:** This city bleeds out into suburbs and smaller towns surrounding it, making it difficult to define where it starts and ends.
2. **Contained:** This city has grown to meet a distinct border and stands out against the scenery.
3. **Planned:** This city was grown with careful thought to strategically preserving and distributing resources while maximizing space.
4. **Condensed:** This city has very limited space and was engineered to take advantage of every cubic inch to pack population and infrastructure.

AGE

Cities grow like people and age like liquor. They trade potential for strength and ability; and slowly their sweetness ferments into a rich and alluring poison. The older a city is the more its problems become its identity. Younger cities lack complicated history and character in kind.

 Roll a d4 or choose one:

1. (1 Eccentricity or 1 Asset)
2. (1 Eccentricity or 1 Corruption)
3. (1 Asset)
4. (1 Asset or 1 Corruption)

1. **Ancient:** This city is the most recent incarnation of a place that has existed almost as long as civilization itself.
2. **Historic:** This city has hundreds of years of history built into it and has seen a few different incarnations.
3. **Modern:** This city has only been around for a few hundred years and has more or less always been the same place.
4. **New:** This city is less than one hundred years old, built as intentional industrial development.

WEALTH

Cities are characterized by their relationship with wealth. Every city depends on a foundation of wealth and industry to form. The way those resources are allocated determines how a city looks and functions.

 Roll a d4 or choose one:

1. (1 Corruption and 1 Asset)
2. (1 Asset)
3. (1 Eccentricity or 1 Corruption)
4. (1 Corruption)

1. **Opulent:** Some of the wealthiest people and entities in the world spent staggering resources to develop this place. It is full of dazzling wonders and extravagant indulgences.
2. **Conspicuous:** This city has been home to profitable industries throughout its history. That has resulted in truly impressive collective achievements, monuments, and institutions.
3. **Fading:** This city was once home to a vibrant industry that has disappeared or dramatically waned. There are monuments, institutions, and infrastructure starting to deteriorate.
4. **Absent:** Whatever resources used to exist in this city are now gone. Aging infrastructure either struggles to function or lies completely dormant.

TRAITS

The choices you made are tied to the **assets**, **eccentricities**, and **corruptions** that define your city. Based on your choices, pick traits from the following table:

Asset	Eccentricity	Corruption
• Robust public transportation • A vibrant arts scene • Celebrated culinary districts • Exceptional schools and universities • Access to unique natural or magical resources • Booming industry • Advanced medical care • Accommodations for a specialized profession • Access to natural public spaces • Robust museums and historical sites	• The city is built around inconvenient geography • This city was developed for very unusual transportation infrastructure • The city is built around and above an ancient metropolis • Wildlife and nature are incorporated into the city • This city was the setting for an iconic story or historical event and has embraced that identity • Historical disasters necessitated unique development • This city regularly experiences extreme weather • This city isn't laid out on a grid	• Law enforcement does more harm than good • The cost of living is artificially inflated • Organized crime is powerful • An essential public asset is controlled by corrupt parties • Part of the city has been left to deteriorate • The city faces a massive bureaucratic challenge to enact any change • Civic leadership serves special interests before the populace • Illegal activity is necessary to conduct normal business • Violence is common

✎ **What is this city's name?**

Landmark
In the real world we associate cities with the cool stuff and places inside them. If you see the Empire State Building, you think of New York; the Colosseum, you think of Rome; the Louvre, you think of Paris. Your city needs similar stuff to have an authentic identity.

🎲 6 **Narrow down your landmark to a specific concept by rolling a d6:**

1. Monument
2. Business
3. Entertainment center

4. Museum
5. School
6. Public building

☀ **Choose its history:**

○ New
○ Modern

○ Classic
○ Ancient

☀ **Choose two words to define a style:**

○ Ostentatious
○ Utilitarian
○ Iconic
○ Welcoming
○ Graceful

○ Menacing
○ Rustic
○ Anachronistic
○ Detailed

🎲 8 **Choose or roll two d8 to find the primary materials used to build your landmark:**

1. Metal
2. Stone
3. Concrete
4. Brick

5. Glass
6. Mud
7. Wood
8. Straw

STORY

Finally, you need to know what kind of story those disparate elements are telling.

 Roll two d6:

1. **On a 6 or less**, the story this landmark tells is ugly.
2. **On a 7–9**, this landmark is complicated.
3. **On a 10 or higher**, the story this landmark tells is inspiring.

❋ **Choose two:**

- ○ This place commemorates a historical event.
- ○ This place holds the city's treasures.
- ○ This place will act as a stage for a critical event.
- ○ This place will offer the PCs a gift.
- ○ This place will ask the PCs for labor.

🖉 **What does the landmark look like?**

🖉 **What is this landmark most known for? Who would tell you that information?**

🖉 **When would the PCs visit this place?**

Residents

Cities are full of compelling symbols and themes, but they really need characters to come to life. This part of the exercise will help you create pivotal NPCs to help drive the plots unfolding in your city.

 Narrow down your residents to a specific concept by rolling a d6:

1. Public official
2. Criminal
3. Celebrity
4. Historical figure
5. Hero
6. Ordinary citizen

☀ **Choose an advantage:**

○ Brilliant
○ Influential
○ Wealthy
○ Skilled
○ Principled

☀ **Choose a disadvantage:**

○ Impulsive
○ Cruel
○ Stubborn
○ Foolish
○ Marginalized

6 **Roll two d6:**

1. **On a 6 or lower**, this person is an **antagonist** to the PCs.
2. **On a 7–9**, this person is **useful** to the PCs but at a cost.
3. **On a 10 or higher**, this person is **helpful** to the PCs.

☀ **Choose two:**

- ○ This person is rapidly changing the city.
- ○ This person is in over their head.
- ○ This person needs something important from the PCs.
- ○ This person has valuable information.
- ○ This person has an unlikely goal.

✐ **Who is this person?**

✐ **What kind of allies do they have? What kind of enemies?**

✐ **What is their most memorable feature?**

Event or Rumor

To have personalities cities need to feel "lived in," as though interesting things will happen there whether the PCs are around to see them or not. You want all the ugly secrets, exciting challenges, and interesting opportunities to bubble to the surface as soon as the PCs walk through the gates.

6 Narrow down your event or rumor to a specific concept by rolling a d6:

1. Contest
2. Holiday
3. Power shift
4. Secret
5. Opportunity
6. Threat

☀ Choose a schedule:

○ **Recurring:** This is the sort of thing that happens on a schedule. It might happen annually, a few times a year, or once in a very long while. It is generally expected, either with excitement or dread.
○ **Dormant:** This is something that has existed in the past or generally played out behind the scenes. It is not impossible that something like this could happen, but it is unexpected.
○ **Singular:** This is a completely unique occurrence and is not expected to happen again.

☀ Choose two key groups driving the action and one being affected in the background:

○ **The marginalized:** People who have been pushed outside mainstream society through poverty, tragedy, or prejudice. The city is their home, but it will not see them.
○ **The working class:** The people society is meant to serve but who do not hold a special degree of power.
○ **The remarkable:** People who have extraordinary or specialized powers, education, skills, or responsibilities.
○ **The wealthy and powerful:** People who control the vast majority of the city's resources and institutions. They do not see most of the city, but they control it.

6 **Roll two d6:**

1. **On a 6 or lower**, this event will create a crisis; choose two.
2. **On a 7–9**, this event will change the future; choose two.
3. **On a 10 or higher**, this event will give people what they need; choose two.

- ○ The whole city will be drawn in.
- ○ This creates a special environment that changes expected behaviors and loyalties.
- ○ People will discuss silent truths.
- ○ The city will look and feel different.
- ○ Everything will hinge on a single moment.

Would an outsider know something unusual is happening? If so, how would they tell?

What will be the most significant day for these events?

How can the PCs have an impact on this situation?

Index

About the Author

James D'Amato is the author of *The Ultimate RPG Character Backstory Guide* and *The Ultimate RPG Gameplay Guide* as well as the creator and game master of the *One Shot* podcast and several spin-off podcasts dedicated to RPG gameplay. He trained at Second City and iO in Chicago in the art of improvisational comedy. He now uses that education to introduce new people to role-playing and incorporates improvisational storytelling techniques to create compelling and entertaining stories for RPG campaigns and one-shot adventures.

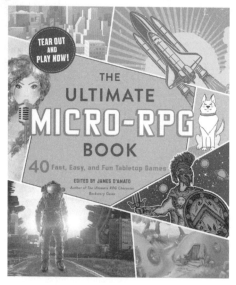